MW01280298

Confessions of a Grateful Substitute Teacher

Barry R Norman

BearManor Media.com

Published in the USA by
BearManor Media
1317 Edgewater Dr #110
Orlando FL 32804
www.BearManorMedia.com

Softcover Edition
ISBN-10:
ISBN-13: 979-8-88771-462-2

Published in the USA by Bear Manor Media

Table of Contents

For Teachers Everywhere

Forward

I do not know why I was asked to write this, but here we are. Actually, I was making a joke by randomly writing something about this book (which I also edited), and Barry said he "loved it," so I, being the great friend that I am, agreed. He also said that I was a "brilliant writer," so why not? This can be my chance for revenge on Barry, since we are frenemies, but I will be kind.

To all teachers and faculty members of any public school who have felt like time-traveling to summer break every year, welcome to the book for you! And to all students who have thought your teachers do not have lives outside of schools, prepared to be shocked beyond belief. Some of your teachers have children, some have traveled the globe, some have beef with you, some want to go home to watch TikTok, and some get stoned every Friday just to forget where they have to be on Monday.

As a substitute teacher, you have to wire your brain to become at peace with your surroundings. If you are a person who loves meditating, do not work in a public school. Most people would believe this book is a comedic retelling of *Abbott Elementary*, except it is not a story of your everyday teacher, but a substitute, and it is a high school. I should mention, he is a real person, not a cartoon villain, although he does occasionally dress like one from *Scooby-Doo*. Another group of people who may enjoy this book are the fashionistas of the world because everything they know will be proved wrong by the iconic fashion statements Barry has made throughout his time in this school. Whoever said hot pink sneakers, germ green pants, and a disco shirt with a doctor's coat is not fashionable has not met Barry. Ok, I am lying, it is not fashionable... at all, however it is the reason we met after I complimented him, kind of, on the "fit.". It is also one of the great strategies for teaching he learned at the world-renowned teaching college... never mind, he did not go to school for teaching, his schooling is almost irrelevant to the situation. Now that I think about it, this was most definitely a choice, both the clothes and becoming a substitute teacher at 60-something years old. In fact, he did not have to read a book about teaching to know what helps students respond, he accidentally stumbled into a clown's closet and came out as one of the most recognizable and popular adults in a school with over 300 of them.

For those of you from a small town, over 300 adults in a school building may sound like a lot, but in this situation, it is not nearly enough. In a school with over 2000 students, staff is needed not just to teach, but to take care of every aspect in the building, whether it be making the lunches so every student is fed, cleaning any accident that may happen (which often does), protecting the school in case of an emergency that seems to be happening very often in this country, or walking around to make sure every student is where they need to be.

When Barry announced he was writing this book, it was explained as a summary about the quirky, strange, hard-working adults that make up the high school located in a small corner of the world. However, what you will find is a shocking and occasionally funny story about the day-to-day world of adults who never left high school. Adults that are trying to make it through a school year that overworks and overwhelms them have their stories told through the perspective of a substitute teacher who bears witness to it all.

School has changed a lot since Barry went to school with the dinosaurs. A meteor and pandemic later, generations of students have lost significant time spent in schools and teachers have lost their patience. Everyone is struggling in the current educational system in different ways, but Barry has lived a life. He's been to the *Olympics*, wrote a handful of biographies, and worked for *Cartoon Network*, which poses the question: What the hell is he doing as a substitute/math teacher/biology teacher/everything teacher in a public school? If you are a *Netflix* or *Peacock* executive, you have been sleeping on this award-winning concept. Quinta Brunson, I think there is a spin-off in the works here…

Finally, to anyone who works in the building that this book is about, have fun with the scavenger hunt!

Nevena Jurisic – World History Teacher

Chapter 1

Turn on the Lights
The Movie's Over

I want to run out of money and oxygen at the same time. Bob Waterfield supposedly said that. He was an NFL quarterback, defensive back, punter, kicker, and return specialist. He played at a time when pro-athletes weren't paid all that much, but he did marry actress and pin-up queen, Jane Russell, and they formed a production company and produced a couple of B films. Thet soon divorced, and Waterfield died at the age of 62, hopefully, on his last dime. His reported statement had been my mantra as I hit my 60's, which I thought would be my retirement decade. I thought that quitting work early was akin to my knowledge of history and wars fought in Russia; how winter came early that year, leading to the defeat of the invading foe. My love of Shakespeare recalled that "Now is the winter of our discontent" and thus at the tender age 62, I thought I reached the winter of my life, discontented or trying to repel an invasion of dying brain cells and diminished stamina. What the hell was I supposed to do now? I had no more plans, schemes or ideas of anything I could get into that would give me the satisfaction of being a business owner, especially a business connected to my love of film, television or sports. I had seen the downward trend of film distribution with streaming services and their release of product "day and date" with theatrical releases was forcing me to put my personal money into the business more and more. It wasn't a planned sell, as I believed I would be running it for many more years, but streaming services meant that the alter cockers who made up the majority of my demographic, had discovered the joys of staying home on their sofas and Lazy-Boys, instead of the uncomfortable seats and even front row couches, disguised as seating in my theater, that had decades of farts and God-knows-what permanently baked into them. They also liked hitting pause to make one of their dozen or so trips to the loo or hitting rewind when they couldn't hear something, instead of looking to their companion or seat-next-to-them stranger, should they be attending stag - pestering them throughout the film and saying things in what they thought was their movie theater voice, "WHAT DID HE SAY???" or pointing at the screen and whispering, "SO, WHO'S THAT GUY?" I was somewhat amused at all the customers who unknowingly were doing their own imitation of MST3K to the chagrin of other customers who weren't privy to the joke.

I also lost my dog, Scooter, after 17 ½ incredible years. He was diabetic and blind, so it wasn't a shock when it happened. He was my last, remaining family member and I was able to take him to work with me every day, where he supervised me as I sold movie tickets and concessions for 9 years. He became such a favorite that townsfolk called him the Unofficial Mayor of Brunswick, ME. Stores in the downtown area stocked his favorite treats knowing that we would come in, and I might buy something there as he snacked away. It hurt too much to stay in that theater without him, especially when customers would bring him up and some insisted to me, "You must get another dog. That's what he would have wanted." When I snapped at an older customer who had recently lost her husband by telling her, "You should get married again. That's what your husband would have wanted," I knew it was time to go.

Depression was lurking again, like a private dick in a classic movie, skulking around a hotel, looking for unmarried couples trying to con the clerk for a room. It seemed like the time to unload the business, which I did at a fraction of what I paid for it due to my imbecilic rush to buy a theater, and the one I ended up putting my hard-earned shekels on was the least expensive theater I had visited and pored over the financials but not nearly enough to be considered due diligence. In infamous, 20/20 hindsight, it was still a sucker's bet; being ensconced in the back of a very weird mall in Maine, having just a single screen and the office's ceiling was only 5'5" high; a foot shorter than my soon-to-be-shrinking frame, and the greedy, commercial property developer (redundant, I know) who owned the mall, his face turning red, yelled at me during our first meeting when I requested a longer-term lease than the paltry three-year one he was offering. The weird, shoehorned-in-a -strange-mall had that goofy, Judy Garland, Mickey Rooney, "Let's get the gang together and make this work" vibe, only I *was* the gang, but dang if I didn't make it work. Undercutting yet another, Jewish stereotype regarding financial acumen, what I ended up getting for it made it a deal on par with Seward's Folly. Without owning the building, the entire sale was based on the FFI (furniture, fixtures & equipment), and the theater's good reputation. I crowdfunded for the top pf the line projector, and invested into a beautiful digital marquee, but when you need to make a quick sale, and your business is in a field on the downturn, you don't have any leverage. I prayed to the Gods of senior living that my retirement investments would be sufficient to call it a career, assuming that Bob Waterfield's quote would be true for me. After all, I had always lived frugally, never indulging in anything that could be considered frivolous, or even smile-inducing. I was never a wine, women, and song kind of guy. I developed a weird reaction to alcohol, where one beer or glass of wine would make me immediately drunk, hungover and pass out, all in the space of 30 minutes. Once I hit my 50's, women found me repulsive, as part of the 6 stages of Man's Allure to Women. Singer, songwriter Leonard Cohen, a genius in every meaning of the word, claimed that we started off in life as "irresistible," and then you become "resistible." Up next is the joy of transitioning to being "transparent," which he described as not being invisible but it's like you're being seen through old plastic, or a lime Jell-o mold. After that, you take that nosedive into the "repulsive" stage. The good news is that you finally morph into "cute," which is often accompanied by "doddering." Hopefully, I have that to look forward to unless I'm already there and nobody told me. In the meantime, I was firmly entrenched in the repulsive stage as the only woman who even looked at me twice was someone I referred to affectionately as "Crazy Banker" whose story would be better suited for another book, as it will have to wait until she shuffles off this mortal coil or moves to Canada as she is all mobbed up, and I don't want to end up with a horse's head in my bed or sleep with the fishes or any other, ghastly end having to do with living creatures and nocturnal activities that we all learned from watching *The Godfather* (1972). The final epitaph to my Trader Jack days was how I spent $15,000 on my living room sound system two years before I bought the theater. I didn't think that purchase through and as the components were proprietary. I have had to spend an additional $10,000 after two of the components broke down, forcing their replacements just to keep me in tunes, making me long for the days of the all plastic, close-and-play record player you could buy in the 60's for something like $15 and get your records from the back of cereal boxes. I just sold that system on eBay for the grand total of $550. but of course, I'm the guy that used his baseball trading cards as a fake motorcycle engine by clothes-pinning them to the wheels of my bike to get that Harley sound instead of saving them where they would be worth righteous bucks today. What I spent on not having a "pitiful, portable picnic player" to play my "fuzzy warbles on,"[1] I saved elsewhere, as I wasn't into fancy cars, or bought a house that would have a vacuum hose attached to my bank account, and I was never a fashionista, preferring my collection of T-shirts, and that one pair of genes I could rely on (Editor's note - that will change, This is called foreshadowing). I prepared and ate the same sandwich/protein drink/chips lunch every day at work, 6 days a week, and my breakfasts and dinners were on a rotating system; *If It's Tuesday, This Must be Belgium* (1969) waffles and spaghetti, so I could budget my monthly food bill and spend the least amount of time in the local Hannaford's Supermarket. In the 9 years I owned the theater, I went on one

---

1   Dialogue from the film *A Clockwork Orange* (1971)

vacation, to Amsterdam, where I found cheap tickets, a low-cost and decent Airbnb, and I had a friend who lived there, nice enough to pay for many of my dinners and show me around the Real Amsterdam, avoiding all the expensive, tourist traps Americans love to visit when in Europe. Powerwalking through the Red-Light District was a huge help.

It all seemed to be lined up. In a few years, I would be eligible for Medicare, Social Security, and all the other discounts that go with becoming a useless Portrait of Dorian Gray senior citizen. I would simply age disgracefully until I became nothing but a shadow and disappear. I had no family at all, so zero obligations to any blood relatives, and my few remaining friends lived a minimum of 1000 miles away. I saw retirement as doing what I had already been doing for years; wake up early, work out, eat dinner around 4 PM and then go to bed where either joint pain, night terrors or the need to pee would rouse me from at best, a light sleep. It would all be the same ole same ole except that I didn't have to go anywhere, do anything or see anyone. I would be free from any responsibility or fun of any kind. I could work with that. I already had decades of practice.

I never thought of being a teacher in my life, unless you count imparting dog tricks to wonderful creatures who will do anything to please you as teaching. Maybe it had something to do with all those ditties we used to say in school such as the famous Alice Cooper refrain from "School's Out:"

No more pencils
No more books
No more teachers'
Dirty looks

Teachers were thought of as "the enemy," and the height of punitive authority to be despised and never emulated and certainly not a career choice. There were other sayings around then such as, those who can't do, teach. And those who can't teach, teach gym.

Hell, even Charlie Brown's animated cartoon specials reduced teachers' voices to a pathetic, trombone wah wah wah wah! And Pink Floyd put the final nail in the coffin for people like me when "Another Brick in the Wall" from their album, The Wall came out in 1979 - my final year of college:

We don't need no education
We don't need no thought control
No dark sarcasm in the classroom
Teacher, leave them kids alone
Hey! Teacher! Leave them kids alone!

I never had anyone in my family that was a teacher except my stepmother, who had the exact same effect on me as Cinderella's had on her. Her only saving grace was that she was an art teacher which was OK. They were the ones that showed us how to have fun with uncooked macaroni, construction paper and glue, but I only saw her as wicked, so she was no role model for me to follow. There were teachers and professors throughout my educational career that I fondly remember, but it just never occurred to me to even think about it as a vocation. The closest I came was when my favorite professor during my master's program in Film Studies told me that of all the people, he's had in his 40 + career, I would be the one whose lectures he would like to hear. Of course, I was in my early 50's during the program and age and experience might have made me more of an interesting person than most of the kids that passed through, who were obviously much younger than me. I thought about it for a moment, teaching film at a college or university, wearing a jacket with elbow patches and mesmerizing the pretty coeds who would flirt with me as they did Indiana Jones in his first film. Nope. I chose to buy a movie theater instead. I wanted to be closer to the art and be the conduit between the artist and the audience. And the type of films I often showed were teaching the audience somewhat. Films like *The King's Speech* (2010), *The*

Imitation Game (2014), *The Theory of Everything* (2014) and *Argo* (2012) were periods in my Baby Boomer's lives and they came away learning more about the event and people involved then they did go in. Owning a movie theater in a small town, you become somewhat of a minor celebrity, which is a nice consolation prize to the fact that the theater barely made enough money to keep it and me going. I never let money influence me regarding my choice of careers. I needed to have passion with what I did to make all the hours of your life it consumed worth it. Now that it was all over, I wondered if my money and oxygen tank were in sync or even talking to each other.

Chapter 2

Love That Dirty Water

I didn't exactly move to Boston, but I did come back "home" to Massachusetts. I firmly believe that if you live long enough, you run into your own delusions and my delusions were that I had trodden the Earth long enough to make mortal enemies or at least piss off enough people to feel uneasy. Thus, I am not going to give exact locations of where I was or am, and I'm not going to use real names, not because I am afraid of offending anyone, or of being sued, but there are obviously children involved and many hard-working educators who sacrifice and they need to be protected from public scrutiny. Someone who isn't discussed here still might see themself in a person I describe so digression gives us both plausible deniability. I am completely aware that if someone really wants to track you down and get you, the internet gives you a load of options for doing exactly that. I'm just trying hard not to poke the bear. Now Massachusetts might not have been the best choice to choose retirement as it's not known as "Taxachusetts" for nothing. It did check a bunch of boxes - proximity to the ocean (did you think I was going to slip up and tell you just HOW close I am to the ocean so you could triangulate my position??), great pizza, and first-rate healthcare. That description also fits New York, Italy, Greece and maybe some enclave in New Zealand but I lived in New York a couple of times before and I did work in Italy for a month and, you know what? I should have picked Italy. I've watched all the Godfather films and *Goodfellas* (1990) enough to imitate a good, Italian American, mobster accent, although it is unclear if that would be helpful.

It wasn't really my old stomping grounds, having never physically or intellectually considered myself a stomper. It was a city (or was it a town? Keep guessing!) that I never really visited growing up here. I first really saw it when I visited to check out a movie theater I considered buying, and I liked it. I thought it would feel exotic to retire in an area that I never visited or explored while growing up near Boston. It was north (or south. I forgot.) of the city, while people who lived in my zip code as a child headed south (or east) to Cape Cod when wanting to travel to the cool part of the state. It meant going back to apartment living which I always loathed, having hundreds of strangers milling about and doing God-knows-what in the comfort of their own domicile which was only separated by a thin sheet of plaster. Still, I thought it made sense to have a swimming pool and fitness room right there. I often wondered what might have happened if I suddenly keeled over, dead in my apartment, how long it would take for anyone to notice. I had no immediate family that would worry if I hadn't been heard from in a bit. I did carry a laminated card in my wallet with all the numbers one would need to call to inform everyone that needed to know that I was no longer a sentient being. One of the first things I did upon arrival was to purchase my final resting place which was a water-soluble ball to hold my ashes and the ashes of my two doggies, and then Dropkicked Murpheyd into the ocean (any ocean) someplace—anyplace. I've been a burden to a ton of people in life and dammit, I wouldn't be in death. So, say something nice about me during the week of sit shiva, ya bastards!!

There was another reason for moving back. The last year in Maine really kicked my ass, and I felt like Malcolm McDowell's Alexander Delarge from *A Clockwork Orange* 1972) after his former Droogs turned into police thugs kicked the crap out of him shortly after his release from police custody. He was crawling through the mud in a downpour, and thinking again and again to himself, "*Home. Home. Home,*" and then he saw an illuminated sign in front of a house that said "Home," and headed for it, not realizing that he had been there before and the atrocities he and his gang committed while there. It would now be anything but home to him. I was thinking the same thing; I wanted to go "home," even though my home state had been anything but kind to me, which is why I high tailed it 2000 miles west at the first opportunity after graduation. I knew some of the people I went to high school with still lived there, but nobody that I was truly friends with, and I hadn't seen or heard from any of them since our 10-year reunion almost 40 years earlier. Did I think I was going to receive a hero's welcome because the filmmaker, writer, movie theater owner, Olympic Games Manager, music business magnate has come back?? Huzzah! Except for the odd social media contact, I knew none of them anymore and they would have no idea what I did since last we met, nor would they care. I sure as hell didn't. I ran away for a reason or ten. Was this was where I was going to spend my final years, puttering around until I reached Leonard Cohen's "cute" stage? My delusions had delusions.

Thus began my sojourn into the world of retirement. Nothing to do but beat on the kangaroos (That's a misheard lyric from Steely Dan's *Black Friday*. It's actually *Feed all the Kangaroos*, but I like my lyrics better). And don't even THINK of changing the word "on" to "off" before kangaroo. That's just gross) and wait a few years until social security money drops. What could go wrong?

Chapter 3

The Age of Contagion

Things were going swimmingly and then came The Hong Kong Fluey (Settle down. That's a reference to the Hannah Barbera 1974 cartoon than a racist epithet). As my retirement money was in investments, when all the markets tanked, so did my portfolio, and because it was a global crisis, it wasn't like you could just put your money into international markets and be OK. You can't continue siphoning off your retirement money while things are rock bottom or there goes the oxygen thing. I had to get back into the workforce, only, who wants to hire someone in their 60's, whose last employment was owning his own business, and before that—a top tier manager for the Olympic Games?

In the meantime, I breathed a sigh of relief for selling my movie theater when I did, but I did feel sorry for the person that bought it and ended up having to shut it down for 18 months.

In the meantime, employment was no *Easy Rider* (1969). If you wanted to drive for Amazon or restaurant/grocery store delivery, you were golden, but I didn't want to pack the miles on my leased car and my arthritic knees, back, hips, and neck just couldn't take the mileage, either. All that was left was to work at the hotel/motel front desks because allowing THEM to stay open during a contagion was a great idea. What could go wrong with letting people travel from whatever high-level infection rate they came from and allow them to mingle together in a hotel lobby complaining on the wait to get into their virus-y rooms??? Lucky me, I did hotel work back when I was 29, when I went to a year program for the music business and worked at the front desk of a HoJos and an Omni hotel while hoping to one day become REM's live sound engineer which wasn't bloody likely. There were lots of openings, including a couple near where I lived and I nabbed one of those to-die-for hotel, front desk jobs. Lack of hotel experience wouldn't be a filter preventing me from nabbing one of those high in-demand, clerk positions.

Unfortunately, I picked the one hotel that did NOT have plastic shields on the desk to at least give the appearance of protection for their employees from their hacking and coughing guests. They also had no limit to how many nose-running people they would allow in the lobby at one time. As is de rigueur in the hotel game, they would ping-pong me all over the schedule as far as shifts and days off which is sooooooooo good for the immune system. Perhaps all my exposure to diseases from around the world at The Olympics, my international film festivals and far-off travelers to my movie theater, served as an early type of vaccine as I was the only one that didn't contract Covid, while my fellow employees were the creatures from Mars depicted in *War of the Worlds* (1953). I was in much demand to run the front desk solo, for every shift I was willing to do. Demand isn't the right word. I was their only option most days. The GM would always hide in her office, never daring to venture out and give me a hand during the crazy check-in period that started at 3PM, as she hated dealing with guests and was just fine letting me take all the heat for their wait, especially when the rooms weren't ready to be checked-in yet, due to all the "sanitizing" they had to do. Truth be told, they did less of that than they did pre-Covid. They didn't wash blankets and comforters, barely cleaned the bathrooms, and mold was a constant problem. As the hotel was seasonal and closed at the end of September, my goodbye present was to report them to the local and state Board of Health. The following summer, they came up with an intern program, so that they could get by calling all their employees "interns," and pay them less than we were getting the prior year with the coveted promise of future work for the company. I read many of the comments left on various travel sights. I found one generated by AI, which I have paraphrased as to not give AI anything in print, so screw you, Skynet (this is a general summary based on a cornucopia of reviews):

While the REDACTED NAME OF HOTEL offers a relaxing atmosphere with stunning ocean views, according to some travelers, the experience is somewhat marred by nonexistent cleanliness and maintenance issues. The rooms, while praised for their views, have been criticized for their small size and inconsistent cleaning service. Many guests enjoyed the amenities like the pool and hot tub, although there were some complaints about additional fees.

The service received terrible reviews, with some travelers finding the staff neglectful and rude. Many guests also suggested that the hotel was overpriced for the services and amenities provided and would never stay there again.

While doing a mini victory dance, upon seeing how wonderfully the intern program did, I went back to the job-seeking sites reluctantly. My next adventure was to be a co-manager for a holiday light show. This shit-show is discussed in extreme detail in my previous book, *BAD DAY for GRANDPA. A Collection of Other Stories and Drivel* (2023). Its title is, *THE-NOT-QUITE-NORTH-SHORE-HOLIDAY-LIGHTS-THAT-SOMETIMES-DON'T-TURN-ON-SHOW*. One Amazon review called this story "riveting." To sum up, that gig might have been mildly fun when I was 16, but at this point, it was rubbing the rhubarb the wrong way.

It would take a few more months after the new year to find my next stop, which, once again, turned out to be in the hotel biz. This one was a part-time seasonal job for a combo motel and Inn. It was located on a river and during that summer, it hosted a lot of wedding guests as there were nearby venues that arranged for their ceremonies and receptions. The location was very Zen, and the guests were always in a good mood due to their reason for being there, which made the overall vibe of the place quite pleasant, except for the horror show who was my boss. She was an ugly, miserable ogre, who obviously despised life with every fiber of her troll existence, and damn if she wasn't hell-bent on making those around her as pissed off as she always was. She tried to screw with my paycheck, claiming that when it was late (as it often was) that it was the payroll company's fault and ditto when the checks were shortchanging me of money for hours worked. I demanded an investigation by the said payroll company, and they agreed to conduct one. The read-out was that all errors in paycheck amounts, and lateness were directly due to my boss's input regarding both my hours and submitting it to them on time. The Inn/Motel ended up having to compensate me a lot more than I was owed, since us older fuckers are all lawyered up and I had them by the short and curlies regarding falsifying payroll documents and screwing with money earned/paid. A Jew in his 60's who thought he was retired, but due to an insane pandemic, found himself working for jobs and for people whom he would never have thought of working for on his worst day, is simply NOT the person to fuck with especially when money was involved. You certainly get more litigious as you age, maybe it's because you know a lot more lawyers without ever intending to have them populate your rolodex.

Another thing about working part time was that I found myself eligible for both SNAP benefits and unemployment after every seasonal job I worked ended. I didn't have to touch my retirement investments, which was the whole point for doing those shit gigs in the first place. Retirement investment money doesn't count as income so matter how much you might have; you can still be awarded limited government dough to keep you in the pink. Hey, if I run out of the filthy lucre before I finally retire, it would force me to continually apply for government programs that I and others had contributed to over the decades, so I'm really saving the government and its grateful citizenry money. You're welcome.

I was growing weary of the part-time jobs that paid shit and kept chipping away at my self-esteem and overall mental health. Something would soon change all that.

Chapter 4

School Daze

Online job-hunting is far too like online dating for my taste. The jobs are never exactly what they appear to be, and they both run on the concept, "My non-response IS my response." Your rejections are never explained, and you must dutifully go to the next one not knowing what the hell you did wrong with the previous one, so you're left constantly gussying up your resume in the hopes that you'll be more attractive to that next, hot-looking employer.

I wasn't so much surprised to see an abundance of ads on a job site looking for substitute teachers. I was shocked by my actual interest in them. Back in my day (yes, I'm old enough to start a sentence with that well-worn cliche), the substitute teacher occupied the dirt-end of the totem pole. Even a nerd like me had no respect for the substitute teacher. When they came into our classrooms, they would be welcomed with jeers, laughter, spitballs or worse. If the class was on the first floor, many of us would simply open a window and climb out. We thought that only the worst kind of dorks, losers, or "*neo maxi zoom dweebies*," as *The Breakfast Club's* (1985) John Bender so eloquently put it, would be a substitute teacher or worse, have a dollop of respect for one. Jack Black's portrayal of Dewey Finn in *School of Rock* (2003) was just the latest example of the total lameness of the substitute teacher, even if he became cool in the end. Plus, some of the jobs referred to them as "building subs," and they were full-time, not just a sack full of losers, waiting by the phone to call them in at the last moment when the missy schoolmarm math teacher couldn't come in that day due to nursing a wicker hangover, brought on by the previous day's hijinks from her disrespectful classes. No, these were everyday positions, with benefits, in addition to all the holidays and summers off, making them the greatest part-time job ever. One ad leapt out at me. It was for the high school in the adjacent city where my dad grew up and where he and his dad practiced medicine for decades, getting a reputation in the region as being Demigods. I knew that they both delivered a lot of babies in that city, so there was something of symmetry for possibly working there. After checking a lot of those openings, that city paid the most and by a wide margin. In fact, it would be the most money I had made since I quit a direct mail advertising sales job decades ago. The qualifications seemed almost too light:

Bachelor's Degree
Strong desire to work with students in an urban setting
Ability to work effectively with teachers, support staff, and parents and advocate for children in order to effectively problem solve
Strong interpersonal, communication, and organizational skills and ability to work with all stakeholders
May be eligible for long-term sub position with a minimum of a BA
Strong desire to work with students in an urban setting
Ability to work effectively with teachers, support staff, and parents and advocate for children in order to effectively problem solve.

Other than my dad and granddad having lived and worked nearby, the other thing I pulled from the morass that served as my long-term memory was that there was a peanut butter factory, a candy factory, and a ball bearing factory along the route, going from our house to my dad's office. I was enthralled with both peanut butter and candy factories, but I couldn't figure out what type of person would grow up thinking, "*Yeah, I want to start a ball bearing factory. That's where the money is.*" There probably was a lot of money in ball bearings. I know you pay through the nose when they wear out although I'm stuck trying to think of what I ever bought that contained ball bearings. I figured a car must have them somewhere in the engine. Who can forget the shame and total embarrassment at elementary school during "what kind of work does daddy do?" and your dad struts in front of your friends and teacher and puts on his best, disarming smile while announcing to all that he's in the ball bearing biz. Getting back to the whole job thing, my main thought was that "Of course they need teachers of every size, color and description." Between school shootings and covid, who the hell would want to work in a school these days? The answer was simple - unemployed, hoping-to-retire-soon me, that's who. Yeah, that's the spirit.

I was able to schedule a Zoom interview the following week with their Vice Principal, Audrey Tingledooz and their HR Manager, Tracey Phip (not their real names). The interview began with them telling me how diverse the student body at their high school was, and did I think I could handle dealing with students from third world countries such as Brazil, Central and South America, Haiti, Vietnam, etc. That was a marshmallow question, teed up in my sweet spot. I told them about my Olympic Games experiences, and how my position was to be the liaison for all the international broadcasters at my assigned venue whose networks paid billions to cover the sport. Four of the Games I worked at were overseas, and the crew I had to manage were locals where you had to quickly understand the cultural differences between them and Americans to get the most work out of them, and to give them the most positive experience of you, your country of origin and the Games. Body language, and even head movements, conveyed totally different meanings upon the culture, and you had to be able to decipher them all to be effective and equally important, to not be offensive. I discussed how I founded and ran an international film festival that hosted filmmakers from around the world, whose understanding of English varied from excellent to not a word. I gave specific examples how a tilt of the head upward in Greece had a totally different meaning when exhibited by someone from India. I could tell by their smiles that I crushed that question and that it would just be a formality before I was hired. They were literally gushing over my credentials, and well before the 20-minute interview ended, they formally offered me the job. The filmmaker in me made me pause for dramatic effect and then to show just how cool I was, I flashed them the two thumbs-up sign. I received the contract offer via email within the hour. Welcome to the mad, mad world of public education, and may God, Buddha, Cthulhu, or The Flying Spaghetti Monster have mercy on my soul, assuming I ever had one having spent the bulk of my career in promotion. Dammit son, you're now a teacher, dirty looks and all.

As I was hired a little more than a month after the school year started, there was no orientation or anything to prepare me for the specific nuances regarding how you do the freaking job. There wasn't even a welcome packet with useful items such as a map of the school indicating crucial information such as where all the bathrooms, water fountains and emergency exits were. The school was designed by a firm that had never been contracted for a design-build of a school before and it showed. It was originally constructed to hold 1700 students, and not the 2400 that were bursting through the hallways and classrooms with that number projected to increase annually. The classroom numbers took odd turns, went down secret corridors that linked to the other side of the building, and some numbers disappeared altogether, only to reappear in another part of the school, totally disconnected to where they left off. The building had one elevator that a snail or giant tortoise could beat to the top, assuming they could ascend on a vertical climb. Upon arrival from the always reliable Google Maps, I ended up at the rear entrance of the school, which wasn't open yet, and I ended up walking about a mile before I stumbled on to the front doors, which amazingly enough had a sign pointing out which way to the main office. Once inside, there was no grand welcome, but just smiles from the office managers, who would become a Godsend in my working life, cheerfully handing me a boatload of paperwork. They then spun me around as if we were playing "pin the tail on the new substitute teacher", to get me to tech where I would pick up my Chrome book, spend exactly 30 seconds going over all the idiosyncrasies from that piece of technological marvel, and then it was back to the office (only got lost once) to get my assignment for the day. There was no tutorial on the Chrome book, or even a modicum of a lecture as to how one performs the job. The tech people were young, and clearly overwhelmed with the massive amount of work they had, keeping the computer systems running and teaching Luddites like me how to be semi-literate at computer functions. While not getting any information about important things like how one takes attendance, they went over the steps of establishing a login password, patted me on the back, wished me good fortune and pointed me in the general direction of the classroom I needed to get my happy ass to, to perform all the functions and responsibilities of a now, officially hired and working (Ta daaaaa!!!) SUBSTITUTE TEACHER!!! Before they sent me packing, they did show a little mercy and asked what teacher I was subbing for, so they could tell me what classrooms and periods I would be covering. I thought, TEACH me to take attendance, and I can do it for as long as I'm employed here. It became obvious that the substance of being an effective substitute teacher was on a need-to-know basis, and obviously, I didn't need to know – not yet anyway. Perhaps it was a brilliant ploy to force me and others like me to interact with my fellow by the n teachers by constantly asking and begging them to show me how to perform my job, because nothing cheers up an overworked teacher more than being interrupted be the new hire, with a plethora of computer questions while they simultaneously prepped for their next class while stuffing their unhealthy lunch down their necks. That's pretty much how it all turned out, with the caveat that the computer program from which virtually all of our work flows, has a ton of methodologies to get to each page and function, and that every teacher has discovered their own little path to get there, so if you ask Teacher A how to do something, you'll be shown their steps, and when you totally forget everything they showed you, the next time you need to execute said function and ask teacher B, you'll get a totally different method. I thought that this must have been the inspiration for Alfred Hitchcock's brilliant film, *The 49 Steps* (1935). Ole Alfred must have been a substitute teacher. No wonder his genre became horror.

Just getting to and from anywhere was a Sisyphean task. The students crammed the hallways, in no hurry to be anywhere. Loud conversations spoken in Spanish, Portuguese, Haitian Creole crashed into each other, creating an international, verbal alphabet soup. The girls wore tiny midriff shirts, and literally all of them could have starred in a Russ Meyer film. Both the boys and girls seemed to prefer wearing pajama bottoms except for the girls that preferred lion tamer's pants, that were pre-shredded for a premium price. Masks were often worn as chin straps, and no one had been taught the protocol of coughing into the crook of your elbow rather than your hand, or worse, the air in front of you. I watched billions of Covid spiked viruses, dancing like evil sugarplums around my head, smiling as they searched for an unblocked orifice from which to make their entry. The teachers all had a glazed look of surrender, probably due to the year plus of trying to teach via Zoom, which went about as well as you would imagine.

I finally found the room I would be taking homeroom attendance at, no thanks to the totally illogical room numbering system that some mango-headed dit-wad created from the architecture firm that screwed the pooch with their design in the first place. And yes, I am grinding on that again as after almost 3 years, I still get lost in the building. The only thing that I was told prior to my first assignment was that all teachers had "duty" from 7:45 - 8:00 when HR started, (homeroom, not Human Resources) and that was to stand outside your room and watch the hallway, trying to move lackadaisical students onward to their HR class, and to be on the lookout for any fights that might break out, as that was a major thing once the schools were allowed to open back up again. I discovered that one of the biggest reasons for all the fights was the fact that during the year and a half sabbatical the students had from being physically in-school, a lot of smack was posted on social media, especially by 7th graders, who technically skipped 8th grade and now found themselves in high school. When the smack-talkers found themselves face-to-face with the person they were dissing on Instacrack, or Smartface, or whatever site or app they fancied at that moment, it was go time. It wasn't just the boys that let the fists fly. I quickly learned that the girls go at it at the drop of a . . . well, whatever they drop these days, as hats had been replaced by the ubiquitous hoodie, and they did not know the meaning of quit once they squared off. At least the boys were in the habit (most of the time) of stopping before too much damage had occurred, but not the girls. I was told all this by a couple of teachers who observed how green I was regarding male/female etiquette and decided to school me quickly on the lack of Marquees of Queensberry Rules when a fight broke out, especially between girls, do NOT intervene by getting in-between them, and for the love of God, do NOT put a hand on them, because that could really come back to bite you in the ass with a legal conundrum that could quickly spiral into your termination or worse. That's the main reason I joined the teacher's union, to get the legal help I might need if there was a moment of "J'accuse!!!" Many of the students knew their way around the legal ramifications of school life these days, and some wouldn't hesitate to say, "child services," or any other agency that would chill you to the bone and let you know who really held the power. Leverage was not in our favor, despite a teacher's union support. It just wasn't a rabbit hole worth exploring.

At 8AM, you're supposed to meander into the classroom and start taking attendance. As I had no clue how to do that on "X2," the site that was the lifeblood of the high school regarding all things attendance, grades, and personal information, on students. It doesn't give up its secrets easily to non-techies like me. I thought that I would just have everyone write their names down on a piece of paper and then take it down to the office. I was totally unknown to students and not one student looked up from their phone when I introduced myself as Mr. Norman. When morning announcements came over the PA, not even a glance of interest from anyone to anything that wasn't in the palm of their hand and emitting a strange glow. When the bell for first period rang minutes later, they all filed out like the walking dead, eyes still glued to their phones, ricocheting off each other like balls on a bumper pool table. It was the zombie apocalypse in ratty clothes, hoodies and ear buds.

Chapter 5

Who Are You?
Who Who Who Who[2]

Remember the disaster movies like the *Airport* (1970) franchise, where at the beginning of the movie, you get to meet the passengers or whoever the key players would be during the forthcoming catastrophe, so you can develop either an affinity or hatred for the participants in the passion play and root or jeer accordingly? Time to play that here. Meet my high school's initial passengers and try to guess their overall impact to the story going forward.

First, there was Pauli Cacciatore; mid 30's, balding, and a local boy who had been through the school system as a youngster and new all of the important, district players and the ins and outs of public-school politics. He graduated law school, but decided not to practice and thought that being a history teacher was his calling. He'd been a sub for something like 6 years, was the best of the bunch by far, and was just waiting for a classroom of his own and the promotion to full-blown teacher. You can't swing a dead otter in a school district without hitting an experienced or hopeful history teacher, so his wait continued. If you wanted to know any of the tea in the school, on any level, topic or rumor or anything about being a substitute, Pauli was your guy.

Next, there was Virginia, "Ginny" Murdoch, whom I nicknamed "Gippy" as she was part Goth chick, part Hippie and it was a short train ride from Ginny. She wore black theater jackets and black leather miniskirts with argyle socks and had purple, green or pink streaks in her hair. She was as nice and sweet as they make them, but I also wouldn't have been surprised if she worshiped Satan or was a

---

2   The Who: *Who Are You* (1978)

member of the Church of the SubGenius. It was that unknown that fascinated me. She ended up taking an internship before the school year concluded and rumor has it, she regretted the move which is a shame.

Jamaal Swisher and Curtis Toothacher were a pair, pretty much joined at the hip. They were hired together, and you rarely saw them apart. They were two Black Street guys who loved basketball, talking smack and just grooving on whatever happened their way. Jamaal played at a high level in Europe and was 6 '7," and cut a pretty, intimidating figure but was basically a very, cool cat. Curtis was much shorter, but his love of the game also permeated his very soul. Neither suffered fools much, and if you dared speak out on their turf and didn't know what you were talking about, they would leave you reeling in the burst of their fast-talking insults. I thought they liked me, as I knew something about the game and they were impressed with my knowledge of players that they heard about, but never saw play as I did; players such as Dr. J, David Thompson, Artis Gilmore, Clifford Ray, and Jamaal "Silk" Wilkes. Being 30 - 40 years older than the other subs certainly was a two-way street, as some thought of me as nothing but an old geezer, soon to be talking pure gibberish while waxing nostalgic about "the good ole days" and puttering around the school on my walker or riding around on a motorized scooter a 'la George Costanza during his brief employment at *Play Now* in *Seinfeld*. Others respected my accomplishments and the fact that I was still hangin' and bangin' in the gym and didn't look my age, not by a damn sight. Of course, part of the reason for looking young was the traditionally bad lighting at your average high school. Life is 90% timing, 10% lighting, or the other way around, depending on what you're doing. I knew things, been places, and sometimes, I could hold court while they listened eagerly for how life went down back in the 60's and 70's, and for some of our younger teachers, the 80's and 90's. I would always come to Earth when I did what I thought was a spot-on, Rodney Dangerfield impression only to met with blank stares. Sometimes, I think they felt I was being furloughed from an assistant living facility do the school's desperate need for substitutes and I was scraping the bottom of the barrel. That could be my paranoia talking, which is another, unfortunate sign of aging. You've been around long enough to know that you *should* be paranoid.

Bryan Diddle comes next; the mid 30's guy who was disgusted with everything and everyone. He wore it on his sleeve that he didn't like the job, the kids, his fellow subs, the school, the weather, the traffic, the food, anything. He would let you know just how much money he made as a sales rep for a software company, which begged the question, just what the fuck was he doing HERE? During his duty in the hallways, he would bark like a Marine drill sergeant in old-timey phrases like, *"Put some pep in your step!!"* He was also the defensive backs coach for the varsity football team, and he played basketball in the gym every chance he got and was good enough to earn respect from his fellow gym-rat students who also played. My second day at the school, they assigned me to him, so I could be taught how to use X2 and take attendance and other things about controlling a classroom, but Bryan loved to get face-to-face with whatever rebellious student showed himself (or herself) to him, so he could try to humiliate them with his corny vision about how life used to be and how the current generation just isn't cutting it to his far-Right wing extremist satisfaction. Eventually, a rumor came out that he had an affair with a student, and while I always took such rumors with a giant grain of salt, if there was anyone that might fit the profile, it was him. I don't think it happened, but rumors tend to stick to you far longer than they should even when disproved, and it gave credence to my decision to become a union man for the first time in my life. You just never knew who might be whispering about you in hushed tones that could find the wrong ear.

Priscilla Ford was in her mid-20's and was quite pretty and she knew it. My sister referred to women like that as thinking that they *"shit French vanilla ice cream."* The only time she talked to me was when I discovered that she was writing a book, and I told her I had written 6 (at that time), and she perked right up and engaged me in conversation until I divulged everything I knew about publishing and then I was back to being part of the Great Unwashed once her own book was on Amazon. She might have a great career in Reality TV as she just oozes drama without saying or doing anything.

Last but certainly not least was Yeehaw Stability, the Turkish God of Religion, Philosophy, History and Sociopathy, AKA the Norman Bates of our high school.

I began hanging out in the 2nd floor teacher's break room as I was told by one teacher that it was *"the place to be."* As a filmmaker and writer, I lack the creativity to come up with the personalities and idiosyncrasies of the Gang from the 2nd Floor. There was Lainey – late 60's, short, SPED teacher (that's special education to you). She would enter the room already in mid-conversation with nobody else involved. If you asked her something or tried to talk with her, she would answer a completely different question, or make a sharp, right turn into another, totally unrelated conversation. Her tales consisted mostly of her travels all over the world, or plays, concerts and four-star restaurants she had frequented over the weekend. Children, grandchildren, cousins and people whose connection to her was never truly revealed peppered her frequent, non-stop patter. She would also turn around and leave while you were mid-sentence in a conversation you would swear you were in with her. She was annoying and endlessly amusing simultaneously. Millie, another SPED teacher, also had a rat-a-tat delivery, but her words were sharp, often detailing the many mistakes her husband made in the course of their lives. She could be brutally honest like the time, she looked me straight in the eye, and in front of other teachers, said, *"I didn't like you when we first met. You were always talking about the films you made or the books you wrote, the Olympics you worked for, your movie theater and it just got boring. You're obviously a narcissist."* She wasn't wrong. I guess when I first started working as a substitute teacher, I brought along with me my initial impression of the job from my own high school years which were as far from being the salad days of my life as it got. I must have been trying to give the trite, *"I used to be somebody!"* rap, so I could certainly understand how that could get grating and boring. It reminded me of the time I ran into a former, quite famous rock star as he was stumbling around in Fenway Park drunk, slurring to anyone who would listen, *"Hello, do you know who I used to be?"* I needed to watch for that behavior in myself, and hope that my first impression could be undone if others viewed me in the same light Millie did. Carol was a SPED math teacher, but she at least seemed amused by me and would often laugh at my pop culture references such as when I learned that her daughter was in a dance troupe, I would blurt out of nowhere, the line from *Donnie Darko* (2001), *"Sometimes, I doubt your commitment to Sparkle Motion."* I appreciated that she found it funny no matter how many times I repeated it to her. She exudes being a great mom and teacher. Peter was the rogue sheltered history teacher; sheltered meaning his students spoke little to no English. His wit was as quick as mine (according to opinion, mine), and he had great timing and delivery in his put-downs and snark often directed my way, which I appreciated. He was something like Robin Williams from *Dead Poets Society* (1989), as there wasn't much, he wouldn't do to get his students' attention, including standing on the desks. He had a small, white board outside his classroom where he would write a different Zen philosophy saying each day. He was heavy into jiu-jitsu, and there was always a slight undercurrent of competition between us regarding how the other would fare if it ever came down to a physical confrontation. He was younger, faster, and confident in his abilities to cause major damage to the human body with his knowledge. I was much older, bigger, and stronger, and I knew enough never to let it out regarding what type of fighting styles I knew and how I might utilize them. It was an unspoken game of the dozens where our challenges were always in subtext, but never overt. I really liked Peter. I have no doubt that he would agree that I really do and should like Peter. Without ever witnessing him in the classroom, I felt that he was probably one of the more respected and effective teachers in the building. His voice bellowed through the hallways during his lectures, and if I had a moment, I would stop outside to listen. Lenny was about my age and a large, former Maine fisherman. He caught on quickly to the fact that I had a self-deprecating sense of humor and he never shied away from giving me the needle as he knew I could take it and I would often hand him an opening to give me a zinger. He was also a SPED teacher and he and his fellow SPEDERS would frequently be locked in conversation regarding their caseloads and their IEP's (Individual Education Programs) and how they were progressing and what they could do to improve their students' scores and overall learning abilities. SPED teachers were a dedicated bunch who didn't receive nearly enough credit for their work and patience. Cori was a math teacher who also taught an incredibly valuable course in financial literacy. She was an absolute sweetheart, who always had something nice and encouraging to say to her fellow teachers. The room always brightened when she walked into it. It sometimes made me wonder if she was on something, but she wasn't that type, and if she were, more power to her as it worked. Hopefully, she was just naturally optimistic. Harry taught math or history, I was never quite sure, and he was also about my age (I did find out that I was the 4th or 5th oldest faculty member in the school), who could be curmudgeonly and blunt when he was unhappy about something. It wasn't that he was wrong with the things that made him irritable. He was just more vocal about them. He had probably seen enough over his decades of teaching to be burned out, but still showed up every year, and I don't think quit was in his vocabulary. Eileen was a science teacher who was also a union rep, and her energy level was either sky high or in the toilet depending on what was going on with the union and the district, as there was always something percolating with either one. She was easy to talk to, a very good listener, and was always appreciative of my efforts whenever I had to sub for her class. Li Quang was the young, cute-as-a-button (if you really find buttons cute; maybe the expression meant Red Buttons??) who was tiny and had roller coaster emotions. This was not exactly diagnosing her as bipolar but when she entered the breakroom, she was either hyper, laughing, and willing to talk to anybody about anything, especially if it was dirt on a fellow teacher, or she was silent, glum, and barely grunted acknowledgement when said hello or ignored you altogether. She was a tenured SPED teacher that was a co-teacher for her classes, and she had a major, laziness streak. She would often slip away from her classes and just let her co-teachers go at it alone, while she went over the minutiae of her OCD, written schedule, or snacked, or just sat, enjoying not being in a classroom. As she did have co-teachers, it wasn't like she was abandoning her classes and students, which would have been a major no-no, and to be fair, her co-teachers could also have been using the advantage of having another person in the class to sneak away, only to a different break room than the one Li frequented. She was constantly looking at clothes to buy online, or she would come in on Mondays and say how she spent the weekend at the mall shopping, but obviously didn't buy anything. She had only about four or five outfits that she would rotate to the point where I could accurately predict what outfit I'd see on any given day. She would also be in some major drama with me that first year. Franco was a rail-thin, gray pony-tailed, Paisano, sheltered bio teacher, who grew up in the district and taught there for a long time. He was in his 70's and apparently thought that the district was more of a mob territory than an actual school district. That came out when the current school superintendent was being ousted by a group, led by the city's very Italian mayor. When I asked Franco's opinion about it, he leaned over the break room table, scowled and growled, *"You don't need to fucking know!!"* This took me by surprise and when I started to ask why, he just repeated it, but with an even angrier tone. I told him that as an employee of the school system, I had a . . . he didn't wait for me to finish. He just said again, *"YOU DON'T NEED TO FUCKING KNOW!!!"* When I continued to protest, he added the line, *"What are you, stupid?? YOU DON'T NEED TO FUCKING KNOW!!"* Yup. Mob talk from someone protecting the territory from a perceived outsider. Franco would probably go to the mattresses if it ever came to that. Talking more with him that year, I found out, to no surprise, that he was a hard-right, conservative, and very religious to the point that he believed in Creationism, which made me wonder how he could be a biology teacher, but then again, about that, I didn't need to fucking know. He probably had friends like Luca Brasi so no sense kicking that dead horse or poking the bear. I had no desire to sleep with the fishes.

On the flip side to that coin was Mitch Blumstein, one of my few, fellow Jewish teachers. He was every Jewish stereotype as far as looks. He was your dentist, your lawyer, your pediatrician, your accountant, your rabbi. In fact, who he really was; one of the country's top cybersecurity experts. He was always winning awards and he would regale you with stories and dozens of pictures from his latest awards banquet. We had a lot in common, especially in music and our knowledge of Yiddish. We would often call out to each other, a phrase from Mel Brooks, *Blazing Saddles* (1974); "*Loz im geyn,*" which meant, "*Let them go*" from the scene where Mel Brooks, dressed in full Indian Chief regalia, comes upon the horse-drawn wagon with "*schvartzes,*" which is Yiddish for black. When we weren't discussing King Crimson or Yiddish, Mitch would show us lots of pictures of his special needs son at a Celtics game as they were both huge fans, and Mitch had season tickets or connections as he was always getting hooked up with cool stuff. The love and devotion he has for his son was touching. Mitch was a true mensch.

Two other major players in the 2nd floor break room didn't join us until my second year , but to delay discussing them until a future chapter would be a disservice. Kylar was an engineering teacher who from the beginning never held back on giving his opinion unsolicited. He was older than I and had a ton of experience in different school systems, so it wasn't like his ideas were uninformed, but he felt he knew how to fix everything. He was probably mostly right, but it could be all part of the delivery. He had a poor opinion of his students, was a tough grader, and the feedback I got from them when I subbed for his class, well, it wasn't great. He could also be a bit of a Human Resources nightmare, given some of the comments he would make to or about women. It was obvious that he meant nothing to them, it might have been that he was coming from a different generation and just hadn't acclimated to the new normal about what you could and couldn't say. I imagined that he referred to any female employee at a cash register as *"honey."* I still kind of liked him. His marriage was still going after many decades so that speaks volumes to the type of man, he must be that we don't often see. Robbie was the 2nd person from year 2 needing mentioning, as his duration was short but incredibly memorable. He was a large, bald man with a deep voice who played offensive line for a division 1 school and could have gone pro if his knees hadn't given out. He also had a long career in the trenches, including a stint at one of the most dangerous schools in the state, regarding gang violence, weapons in school, and students who will fight to the death over nothing. According to Robbie, that school's administration was one of the evil and corrupt you could imagine, with threats, coercion, bribery, and thievery being the norm. He would come to school almost as early as I did, so we would be alone in the break room, and he would regale me with the most vicious and violent stories you could imagine. It sounded a lot like a mob movie, especially with the nicknames everybody had, such as *"Spuds Budney,"* or *"Greasy Thumb,"* and *"Baby Shacks."* He was no stranger to violence himself, and many of his stories ended with him laying somebody out, which he would describe as a matter of fact as if it was no big deal to him. They probably weren't. Just another day in the neighborhood. The stories never ended, and most of the other teachers, especially the women, would flee when he came into the break room. He became *The Demolition Man* - killing all conversations when he walked into the room. I listened dutifully because with all the violence and gangs showing up at his school, armed to the teeth, he still came off as a nice guy as he too, was a SPED teacher. The violence, fights, corruption, bribery, blackmail, and all other instances of evil were just a part of his life and always had been. They became no big deal to him, just the way the cards were dealt. I listened and clenched my teeth and wondered how anyone could survive such a life. Suddenly, he was absent for a long time. When he returned, he said that he was having problems with internal bleeding, specifically from his scrotum where sometimes, blood started shooting out of him as the alien did from John Hurt's stomach from the eponymous movie. It was ghastly listening to his detailed descriptions of what he was going through, and all the ER visits, he obviously wasn't right when he returned, as he was walking very gingerly. He ran out of medical leave and personal days, so he was forced to return. That didn't last long. He was down in the cafeteria and the water cooler needed replacing, so he tried to lift the large, heavy bottle himself and his leg slipped on the puddle below him, and everything split open again and he had to leave. We learned that he died a few days later after that incident, but we weren't informed until weeks later. No one has spoken about him since, and there was nothing about him in that year's yearbook. They kept his picture in the school's website section where it showed every department's faculty member or perhaps no one thought to delete it. I thought it sad to see that picture there, with nothing about his short but memorable time at school. I saw him as a man with a violent past who made the conscious decision to put his life towards a completely different use. Regardless of his blood-curdling stories, I thought about what it took to become a SPED teacher, and however he came off to people due to his gruff exterior and hard-to-listen stories, the fact of his chosen vocation should trump any other impression people took away. He was one of us and he should be missed.

Two more people need to have their introductions here. The first would be Principal Dave Bowman. He was rather an odd duck, the proverbial puzzle wrapped in an enigma. He wasn't built like a duck, rather a penguin, and he lacked, for my money, any level of communication skills. He never answered emails, and he sometimes called for meetings of the subs in his office, minutes before they were to take place, which pissed those of us off who had plans or a dental appointment or some such thing. Whenever we had staff meetings in the auditorium, he would have a guest speaker regarding some issue he wanted to address. Principal Bowman would always lead off and speak, only to have his guest speaker totally contradict virtually everything he just said. He had gone through the district as both student and teacher and he really did seem to care for the students, so much so that he obliterated virtually every form of discipline the school had and thus tardiness, absenteeism, cell phone use, and fights reached epidemic levels. It might have been that he felt they had been through enough due to Covid which was understandable, but he really hamstrung the teachers in our attempt to curb those bad habits. He would end every day over the PA system, telling the students not to congregate in front of Walgreens, or go to a nearby park as fights often broke out there, which of course, increased the likelihood that would be exactly where they went and what they did. Tell students from any generation not to go somewhere or do something and there is nothing else that they would rather do and no place else they would rather go. He loved standing at the front doors when school began, so that he could greet the kids, or he just saw it as a PR opportunity to make sure that he was seen doing his job. Summarizing my impression of Principal Bowman, I would say that he was a decent fellow who did care, but he was overwhelmed by the post Covid realities of running an urban school with a large immigrant population, and he was relieved of his duties at the year's end after a 14-year run. They did it in typical fashion, "reassigning" him to be head of the custodial department or something as unfathomable, knowing that he would refuse and leave the district, which he did. I heard that he was appointed principal in a school located in one of the state's worst districts.

The other fellow that bears mentioning is Carlo Pastafazooli, who is a success coach which is a fancy name for hall monitor, which is not meant to be pejorative. Principal Bowman had rid the school of a team of people who oversaw security in the hallways and throughout the school, and when things kept getting out of hand, he hired a small group of success coaches to take over those duties, although I never understood the title, "success coach." They would roam the floors to make sure that the students were in class, and if they were in the halls during instead, they better have a pass issued from a teacher. Bathrooms were a gathering place for wayward students to escape class, vape, or do whatever they wanted to do except be in their respective classrooms.

Carlo and I hit it off immediately. He was into puns and making a joke out of the joke you just made. I made the mistake of letting him be one of the few people who knew I had a PhD, due to my dad making me swear not to introduce myself as such as he thought my PhD in film studies wasn't nearly the same as the MD, he, his younger sister, and their father earned. Whenever he saw me walking towards him in a hallway, he would say loud enough for all to hear, "*Paging Dr. Norman. Paging Dr. Norman!*" It got old quick, but I had to admire his refusal to let go of a gag once he decided it was funny. He also ran a podcast with a friend of his and invited me to be on it, due to my fascinating background as a filmmaker, movie theater owner, and writer of several books. We had to do it on Zoom, and Carlo gave me instructions to duck at the start of the show, so the camera didn't pick me up until they introduced me, and then BAM! I would spring up, and my big, fat face would suddenly be seen by the one or two people who were watching it when it aired later on local Public Access Channel. I did that and listened to 15 minutes of the worst Borscht Belt comedy that two non-Jews ever attempted. They were trying to comment on the news of the day, but it sounded more like your two weird uncles, kibitzing during Thanksgiving dinner after a glass or two of Manischewitz. Finally, I heard his partner start to introduce me and mangle all the facts I sent him about myself. By that time, my neck and back were aching from bending under my kitchen table for so long. Other than that, the podcast was, well, there's a reason why everyone has one these days. Because they can.

Chapter 6

Taste the Rainbow

It was frustrating seeing scores of students wander the halls, head down, staring into their phones. During the classes I was subbing for, I would walk around, and see if I could find someone, anyone who would engage with me, but there were rarely any takers. The fights continued to rage on in the hallways, the cafeteria, and I assumed at Walgreens and the local park they were warned away from by Principal Bowman. I felt that I needed to try something to shake them out of their stupor, if only for a day or just that moment. I had a pair of bright, purple sneakers that I only wore when I worked out, and I thought, what if I bought purple pants, purple socks, and a purple shirt and wore that to school? I thought maybe it might bring at least a momentary grin to a few faces as they pointed and laughed at The Purple Haze, or Barney, or The Flying Purple People Eater, or whatever the hell else they thought of me. I didn't care if they thought me an idiot, as long as it had a reaction that took them out of themselves just for that moment. I found everything I needed online and wore it one day for the experiment.

I was shocked.

Not only did it get smiles galore from both students and faculty, but many high-fived me as they passed and several commented, *"Nice drip, sir,"* or *"Nice fit."* I had no idea what "drip" meant, as it had a very negative connotation back when I was in high school and could lead to a fight as it was just another way of saying that you had a very large stick, protruding from your sphincter. Students didn't just do a walk-by high five or comment but stopped to engage with me. They asked me about my "drip" and what was up with that, and soon, they began asking questions about ME, and not just the clothes. And it continued that day in the classes I was subbing in. Many would talk to me or respond when I talked to them as if we were real, human beings. My roaming in the classrooms led to discussions, and I told some about my background as a filmmaker, movie theater owner, writer, and even my brief stint in aviation, which stirred as many, if not more, questions than film, TV, and music. The movie theater owner pricked quite a few ears up, and they immediately asked what I got from the sale and assumed that I must be rich, and those conversations could go on for a while. One student went to her computer and found the P&S (Purchase and Sale) agreement from a government site in Maine, and I thought that would kill the "Sub is rich" talk, but the amount was huge to them, and that kept things going. I found, nay stumbled onto something, a connection, a way in. I had to keep that going.

Once you buy a certain kind of item online, the algorithms kick in and you will be inundated by sites that sell similar clothing on all your social media. If I entered something in the Amazon browser, such as, "multicolored pants," or "rainbow shirt," not only would a plethora of them show up on Amazon, but tons of other website stores would pop up on my feeds. You had to be careful as many of them were scams, but I found one, Chinese site, Light-In-the-Box, that sold these cool hoodies with laser-prints on the front and back with incredible colors or scenes from the universe, or dragons, or whatever your fancy. I also had a couple of Hawaiian shirts already, and when I wore those, a teacher named Skip French, who was an aficionado of Hawaiian shirts, informed me what they must have to be considered official Hawaiian shirts. The design on the pocket must blend seamlessly with the design on the shirt and the buttons must be made from coconut husks. He told me about a company that was no more, Paradise on a Hanger, but you could only find their shirts on eBay.

I became obsessed. No, that's not correct. I became addicted. I kept buying more and more shirts and pants of every color, pattern, and description. I accumulated enough of each to never have to wear the same outfit twice in several months. Even though I would wear the same shirt or pants again, the ensemble would be different, and people would think that everything was shiny and new. I became iconic. Or moronic. Although I'm not sure there's a difference.

I was getting more than just noticed. I was getting talked about, discussed and often approached. The combination of the clothes, my work background, and the fact that I was in my mid 60's, didn't look like it, and certainly didn't DRESS like it, made me a novelty, and a positive novelty at that. In the time of Covid, a positive novelty turned out to be a good thing, especially in a pressure cooker such as high school. I became fearless. There was no shirt, pants, or jacket so outrageous that I wouldn't buy it or wear it to school. I easily spent well over $1000 on clothes, and my walk-in closet had such a technicolor look, that I called it my "Skittles Collection."

Students didn't just high five me, comment on the drip (my slang increased to include the words "fire" and "slay"), but they started talking and even opening up to me. The first ones to really do that were two freshmen who were boyfriend/girlfriend: Jason and Haleigh. Jason was tall and probably considered an Adonis in comparison to the typical, high school teenager, and Haleigh was under 5 feet, with an angel face and somewhat of a devil personality, probably because she must have been bipolar which came out of our soon-to-be frequent discussions. Within minutes of watching them together, you could see clear signs of codependency, passive aggressive behavior, and maybe even a little bit of histrionic personality disorder. As they told me more and more about their "childhoods" (a relative term), it became somewhat obvious what was causing their behavior issues to each other and on their own; a double dose of abandonment issues by the father figure. They would soon be seeking me out daily, as a couple, and individually. Jason would often email me and ask me what rooms I would be in, as would Haleigh. Haleigh had some serious anxiety issues, and she would ask her teachers for a pass to come to my room, and they started granting them to her as they found that she would calm down quite a bit in my presence which could last for the rest of the day.

Jason began referring to me as his "therapist," and he would tell me much about his life, his abandonment issues and his true feelings for Haleigh. They had a love-hate relationship, where Haleigh would need Jason desperately, and then push him away if she felt him to be too clingy. When either was alone with me, they would become very introspective, and would make some very good evaluations of their own lives and how they might proceed together or apart if need be. I rarely dispensed advice, sticking to an actual psychotherapy process of just listening to them and letting them have their own epiphanies. When Jason would mention some behaviors that might force me required to fill out an official report called a 51A; as teachers are considered mandated reporters and must report all observed or suspected cases of child abuse or neglect or if they are a danger to themselves or others (I have had to fill out several during my time), I would remind him how much I loathe paperwork, which qualified as a joke with major truth behind it.

Several students started using me in the capacity of therapist, coming to my rooms from their scheduled classes. I soon figured out that some of them were using me as a sort of get-out-of-class-free guy if they just wanted to ditch and have someone listen to their high school dramas. One such person was Lucy, a girl from Haiti, who would always tell me that she wanted to kill herself, or that she had tried multiple times, and her parents kept either sending her to a psychiatric hospital or threatening to do so. I felt the need to confer with both her guidance counselor and school therapist to see just where all this stood, otherwise, I would have been filling out 51A reports every week on her. They told me that while there was a glimmer of truth in what she was saying that most of it was hyperbole as that was her way of getting attention and that the authorities were aware of her as all required reports had been filed. Of course, that didn't mean one shouldn't ever take her seriously. I discovered over time that she was just a typical teenager of the time on psychological PEDs. Everything was taken to 11, and all the normal, teenage angst she displayed was just her way of dealing with life. I stopped allowing her to just come to my classes, but I kept our relationship going by continuing to listen to her whenever we ran into each other. I would not want to drop the ball and ignore something she said or felt. Even the boy who cried wolf could encounter a wolf at some point. She did amuse me with her hopes of being filthy rich and her plan to accomplish it was to meet some, random rich guy who would take her away from all this, reminding me of Calgon TV ads from a bygone era. She wasn't the only student with that plan. For those kids, I tried to exhort the idea that money earned was much more satisfying than money gained by a spouse, and that the goal should be to buy your own damn lifestyle. I was never sure that concept was believed or embraced. Hopefully, before their graduations, I will have made some headway, otherwise, I'll have to run into them at yacht clubs, art galleries and major fundraising galas to learn if my lessons stuck. I was afraid of turning into this teacher whose classroom I referred to as The Island of Misfit Students. Brad LaLane was a HUGE man with a gentle soul. A former football player, and law school graduate, he made me jealous by regaling me about his time in LA as a film production assistant and that he hit the jackpot and sold a screenplay about the true story of his coaching a girls hockey team. His classroom was filled with students not scheduled for his law or history classes, but they loved his calming manner and the school had to be aware, but who was going to tell the behemoth lawyer what he could or couldn't do? He reminded me of my high school social worker whose office was the haven for all students who wanted to be able to smoke inside school under the ruse of needing his guidance. Through the haze of his room, guidance was what they received, and if he suffered lung cancer from the massive amounts of secondhand smoke he must have inhaled over the years, quite a few students and their parents owed him a mammoth debt of gratitude for what he did for them. I don't know if that was his fate, but it wouldn't shock me.

Yessica (pronounced Jessica as some incorrectly pronounce the Y as in yes), was another student of which I developed a rapport.

She was, what her fellow Brazilians referred to as a "Brasi" – someone from Brazil who has dyed their hair bright, bright blonde, with the dark roots showing and was just a tad crazy. Yessica had a noticeable aura around her, and she oozed charisma. I had her in previous classes, before the advent of my Skittles turn, but we had never spoken. As I was taking my laps around the classroom, checking out their TikTok videos (I often gave my rant against TikTok, as a filmmaker who works his ass off to make a film, and after a year on the fest circuit, I'd be over the moon if 500 people saw it, while any nimrod can do something stupid, record it on their cell phone, upload it, and get a zillion views and influencer checks), when she looked up at me and smiled. That was all I ever needed to engage, so I started talking to her, asking the typical questions about what year she was in, what subjects she was taking, and what her interests were. She was noncommittal in all those areas, so I tried to press her to find something that struck her fancy, and her reply surprised me based on her previous answers; *"I like psychology and criminal justice."* Whoa! That came out of nowhere, so I pressed her on it, and discovered that Yessica was quite intelligent, despite my stereotyping her for being a Brasi of uncommon, good looks, and lazy attitude. I asked her to hang on for a moment, and I retreated to my desk and looked up her student profile on my Chromebook and discovered that she had quite a few absences and tardies. I walked back to her desk, with a somewhat shit-eating grin, and asked her about all her no-shows and lateness. Her answer was what I expected, school, for the most part, bored her. That wasn't Earth-shattering. Most students were addicted to their phone, prior to Covid, and the isolation during the time away from school deepened their dependence and totally required the neuro pathways of their brains to rely on the dopamine shot they would get when seeing a video, text message, or playing a game they enjoyed. They could no longer handle boredom and would retreat to their phones for their entertainment, their #1 demand out of life, enabled by Principal Bowman's and the school district's totally lax treatment of the cigarettes of this part of the 21st century. She gave me a glimpse inside, with her interest in psychology and criminal justice, which led me to believe that she had a career path in forensic psychology, even if she wasn't aware of its definition. I kept nudging her towards a realization of what it would take to reach that field and how she should plan to get there. She seemed very responsive to this line of discussion, and I told her to seek me out with any questions regarding college (she was a junior) and how she might get there. She would do just that. Whenever we passed in the hallway, or if I had her in a class, we would talk about what I always stressed to every student who would listen; the thing to have in life is options, where you get to choose what you do and where you go, instead of having to settle for the only things available to you. Yessica would send me texts to meet me in the library during intervention periods, and we went over everything, including the possibility of her entering the military to get her college tuition paid. I suggested that she and her mother meet me and a friend who served 10 years in the navy for lunch, so she could get a first-hand opinion from someone who had been there. We became close enough for her to confide in me regarding her personal life. When she texted me one day and asked what you need to do to get a restraining order, I told her that we need to meet in person and discuss. She relayed the entire story of the fight she got into with her older sibling who threw a beer bottle at her, cutting her forehead, requiring stitches. I ended up having to write a 51A report on the incident as there was no way around it. I couldn't ignore that she had been hurt by someone who lived in her home. Yessica was determined not to let anything get her off her path once she became totally aware of it. Her absences and tardies faded into the background and she took her studies seriously and understood that her intelligence was her ticket to the life she wanted, not her looks. She was able to identify what such a life would be like, so it wasn't hard to convince her of all she needed to do to make that a reality. She had also gotten a part time job after school and was quickly promoted to a supervisor position. I knew that Yessica was on her way, showing ambition and responsibility, two qualities that would serve her well. It felt good to know that I played a small part in her new confidence and motivation, and I knew that we would stay in touch enough for me to see exactly how it was going and I felt that it would be a good place. I knew that the Skittles were a big part of why students would even talk to me, let alone let me into their lives to hopefully have a positive influence, but as they say, your uncle can get you the job, but it's up to you to keep it. My clothes helped make the man, but my desire and experience to connect kept them coming to me. They also help you get bumped to first class on airplanes. So, laugh if you want to.

Chapter 7

With Three You Get Eggroll

Yeehaw would sit in a corner of the 2nd floor break room, dressed in a suit, wearing a fedora and a bunch of religious necklaces. He was always reading from the pile of books he always brought with them which were religious, philosophical, psychological, and historical tomes. He had an intense stare that basically told you to stay away, but I thought he just might be shy and buried himself behind his books as a defense mechanism. One day, I decided to approach him, being a fellow sub and all, and introduce myself. He seemed happy that I was making the effort and smiled as he extended his hand to shake mine. I commented on his books, as I was also quite interested in philosophy, psychology, and history. He mentioned that he was trying to write his first book on Thomas Aquinas, which would combine all those topics, and I said that I was a writer who had written several books. He got a little hyper at that news and started asking me all kinds of questions, his most repeated was how exactly you start. I told him that you can't wait for the perfect sentence to come to you, that you just must break the ice and start. Maybe the first sentence you write will be placed much later in the book, but once you get over the fear of writing, it starts to flow and the order that you write doesn't really matter. You can reassemble the book later, or in my case, with my first book, I let it stay in a jumbled-up timeline which I thought made the book more interesting. Yeehaw then called me a "G" which made as much sense to me as drip did, but I asked around and everyone who is younger than me (which is pretty much everyone) said that it stood for God, which really flipped me out. I'm not a God and don't want to be referred to as one, especially from someone I just started talking to. But it got worse from there. When he discovered I was working on a new book, he began delivering these long-winded, nonsensical descriptions about what he thought was going to happen:

We'll go on a world tour together, doing interviews
for our books and you got my back, and I got your back.
And it will be great, and we'll be rich and famous and . . .

It just went on and on like that, going around in circles, adding in a lot of "G's," and I realized just what in the holy fuck I got myself into by just deciding to talk to this yutz. I didn't want someone that nutzoid as an enemy, so I would just smile although I did try to let him know that if he was going to write a religious, philosophical, psychological, history book, chances are that it would be published by a totally different publisher than my satirical book on pop culture, and that if they did sell, there would be no way that we would be booked on the same talk shows or media interviewing writers for their new, best-sellers. I thought I could shoot this talk down by telling him that there are lots of publishers dedicated to religious tomes, and that he had a better chance of not having to self-publish than me based on what his book was about. That didn't deter him, and whenever he saw me at school, I was "G" and we were going on a world tour and that whole got your back thing, and there just didn't seem to be any way to stop it. Until . . .

I had noticed that Yeehaw and Li were often together, talking in the break room or in the hallways, and I knew the look of reciprocal smitteness, but I was also interested in Li, and had asked her out, but she ran from the break room before giving an answer. I continued seeing her and Yeehaw together and thought that they both just might be crazy enough to understand each other, so good for them. Then one day, Li went up to me in the break room and held up a little sign that said, "*I have a boyfriend.*"

I started laughing to myself as I knew that she was referring to Yeehaw, and I also knew that he was too chickenshit to ask her out and was hoping that she would do the deed for him. It went like that for a few weeks. Yeehaw would call me a G and talk about our world tour, backs etc., but also about Li. He was talking about his frustration with Li, but he wouldn't get specific and damn if I was going to ask him for details. Li had stopped coming into the break room, and if I saw her in the hallway and said hi, she would ignore me. I thought that there was probably a three-way link to all that, but I didn't really want or need to obsess over it or even give it a tiny brain cell of my time. Then one morning, Yeehaw came into the break room and sat down next to me in our "corner" and started to trash Li. I gently told him that Li was a friend of mine, and I didn't really want to hear anything negative about her. He stopped and blinked a bunch of times, stood up, and slowly said, *"I'll have to leave and think about that."* And with that, he disappeared for the next few weeks. He stopped coming into the office in the morning to get his sub assignment as he pissed off the two black subs by assuming, what he thought, was a hip, Black urban accent, and would talk to them in what he thought was acceptable slang. They told him in no uncertain terms to get the fuck away from them and so he had to have his assignments texted to him from the VP rather than deal with two, disgusted Black men that just didn't suffer fools, even if it meant being called a "G."

Soon after, Li started coming back into the break room, and as we were the first ones there, she would start talking a blue streak, and of course, it was all about Yeehaw. She told me how handsome she thinks he is (I sure as hell didn't see it), but also, how incredibly weird he is (that, I saw). They went out to the New England Sea Aquarium. She showed me a video of them where they are approaching one of the large tanks with turtles swimming about and he said, *"You must respect the turtles."* All I could think of was *"What the fuck does that mean??"* They went out to dinner and back to his house, and I can only imagine that what happened next was akin to how magnets can both attract and repel. It's at the subatomic level and similar to magnets, Yeehaw and Li were both North and South Bipolar. Perhaps they were closer to The Original Star Trek's concept of matter and anti-matter, where the end result of a collision is total annihilation, worse than anything Robert Oppenheimer dreamed of after a night of gas station tacos and Jägermeister. Li showed me the texts between them where they are just blasting away at each other, confirming the Law of Diminishing Returns as the more they let each other have it, the less they seemed affected by it and the cycle would just repeat. There was some real misogyny in his texts. I asked her if he was the reason, she stopped talking to me and she replied yes that he basically forbade her, under no uncertain terms, from interacting with me. I asked her why the hell she obeyed that order, and she got quiet. She showed me a note he wrote with the school classroom master key that she had given him wrapped inside, presented in such a dramatic way, it would have made a heartbroken freshman boy proud.

Yeehaw stopped coming into the 2nd floor break room and Li resumed coming in every morning to talk with me and let the Yeehaw bashing continue, and I bet myself that it will soon reverse itself. And so, it would, back and forth for months. Li would get back in Yeehaw's good graces or vice versa. And I would be the odd man out. Li would ghost me and then come back for more Yeehaw bashing, and then off she would go back to a relationship that somehow would never consummate. I'd be shown a series of texts, notes, or whatever he would leave her to show the absolute, this-time-I-mean-it, end of their relationship until it wasn't the end. You got whiplash trying to follow their on again, oh hell, it's off again nonsense. It was better than any Brazilian telenovela or Douglas Sirk film. It tickled me to no end to bear witness to that lunacy. I had shared code names for them both. When Yeehaw, on his rare moments when I was back in his inner circle, we referred to Li as "Puffs," which was short for "Cocoa Puffs," which I derived from the breakfast cereal whose mascot was an insane bird who would cackle on a seemingly meth-driven rant, *"I'm cuckoo for Cocoa Puffs!!"* In one of Yeehaw's more memorable apologies to Li, he had a bagful of gifts, including a box of Puffs tissues. Li's and my code name for Yeehaw was "Kitty," which was Yeehaw's secret word for ketamine, a drug that he self-administered in order to deal with anxiety, depression, and whatever goblin he had going on in his bald noggin. It helped name one of my books which detailed my lifelong battle with insomnia, as I called it *Counting Kitties* (2022), as the end detailed a would-be experiment, I ended up not taking, at a ketamine infusion center. Puffs admitted that Yeehaw had his own code name for me which was "Barney." When *Counting Kitties* was released on Amazon, there was a one-star review from someone named "Barney." Gee, I wonder who that could have been??

Kitty's mental health affected me in multiple ways. He had been given a long-term, subbing assignment for a teacher that broke her collarbone and was out for 6 weeks. Her class was a reading comprehension class for students with social emotional behavior problems. When one of the students, a large girl with serious anger issues, threatened him, he asked to be taken out of the class; something he did and continued to do his only year at the high school. They asked me to fill in, which I was glad to do, thinking that my writing background would be helpful. I tried to get the kids to read out loud, so that I could judge what their reading levels were, but they refused. I came to the next class with my first book; an autobiography called *Flipping Point* (2016), and I asked them to read from that. I found paragraphs of very personal material about me and explained that to the class that now were all invested in potentially embarrassing scenarios. They agreed and proceeded to enjoy reading from my book, which did prove quite helpful in my assessing their abilities. Even the student with anger issues that chased Yeehaw out of the class came around to me, once I discovered that the main source of her anger was the death of her dad. I shared that my mom passed right after I turned 11, and that seemed to help her trust me and work with me in the class.

Another student from that class, Rachell, didn't show for the first two weeks. I checked her profile, and she was either skipping school altogether or was tardy to virtually every class. I didn't make a big deal out of her showing up finally, but just left her alone to see how she would react. She remained stoic in virtually every class, not smiling, talking, or participating, and I never tried to force her. I would simply try to say very little, except hello when she came to class, and goodbye as she was leaving, smiling for her both ways. This was her freshman year. Now, whenever one of us sees the other in the hallway, we'll rush up to the other to talk. She has been very open and honest with me since then, and recently asked me if I would be at her graduation next year. I told her that we were basically freshman together, and that her graduation, assuming the school kept bringing me back, would be my 4th year too. You're not supposed to become friends with the students, but I say screw that. If that's what happens organically without pushing it, why not? Perhaps it's because they remind me what could have been. I don't have children and my sister never wanted them (she went to her OB/ GYN at 22 to have her tubes tied, but the doctor refused and told her to come back in 10 years. She did and to the day). Their perspective on life is vastly different than mine and I enjoy trying to see the universe through their eyes.

The reading comprehension class was also where I was when the school received a possible credible threat of a shooting. We were first alerted of a "shelter in place," which means we can't leave the classroom under any circumstances, but it's not the level of a threat. It usually means that there has been an accident or illness, and they don't want people milling around the hallways or staircases in case an ambulance needs to get through. Soon, Principal Bowman's voice came over the PA, and announced that we were in lockdown, which means that there has been a threat, and, all doors must be locked, and ALICE protocols would be in place. ALICE stands for Alert, Lockdown, Inform, Counter, Evacuate, and every school staff must become certified in ALICE training. Now, the classroom of social emotional students was a small classroom, and the number of students was 10. Just prior to the shelter in place announcement, they had to fold in a 2nd similar class of 12 students into the tiny room with students that I didn't know. When the lockdown announcement came, it was my job get the door barricaded, and instruct the students to pick up an object to throw potentially at the shooter, if he or she breaches the door; the concept being that while they are fighting off staplers, books, or whatever we can hurl, we rush them and get the gun and the shooter down. In the meantime, everyone must spread out around the room and keep deathly quiet. With two classes of emotionally disturbed students who didn't really know each other, that wasn't happening. They were on their phones loudly, even with my orders that they must keep quiet, and a couple of students melted down, crying. My main job at that time was to do all I could to calm them down and assure them that we will be all right, and to just keep still so no one knows anyone was even here. I turned out the lights and put up a large cloth I found over the glass part of the door, so that you couldn't see in. Lockdown lasted just over two hours, and after we were able to evacuate the room after the police gave us the all-clear sign, most of the students ran out the front doors, crying where most of their parents were waiting for them, most as hysterical as their children.

Many months later (I forget how many), Li told me that Yeehaw mentioned to her that he wasn't in school that day and said that he could have been the one that made the call, but he couldn't remember doing it if so. I told her that she should go to the police and report it. They could check his cell phone activity to see if it was the one that called the school at the specific times they had. She didn't want to get involved and I was loathe to report it based on hearsay and basically force Li's hand into becoming a potential witness. I still wince when I think about not at least trying to see if the threats were, in fact, made by Yeehaw/Kitty.

Besides the twisted doings of the triangle that was Li, Yeehaw, and me, year one ended with a bang, not a whimper. As most subs were, I was assigned to proctor a final exam. Exam proctoring was easy work. It was the only time students gave up their phones willingly and they were deadly silent during the exams. Plus, there really was no way to cheat, unlike the tutorial you got during the final exam scene in *Fast Times at Ridgemont High* (1982), all done to the Jimmy Buffet tune, *I Don't Know*, which was just Spicoli's Theme recycled. There was no acting like Mr. Hand and taking off sunglasses, to see if a student was high, or roughly grabbing a cheating student's head and wrenching it around away from the kid they were cheating off. No, it was just fiddling around on the computer while they languished away, swearing at themselves under their breaths for not paying attention when the material was being taught. Suddenly, I heard a girl's voice say, *"Sir? There's a fight going on outside our room."* I took a quick look through the door glass, and sure enough, two girls were wailing away at each other. I sprang to action, not sure what the hell I should be doing. One was crouched down in a fighting stance and popping her opponent with sharp, right jabs to her left eye, while the other was using her right hand as a jackhammer, slamming it on top of the crouched girl's head, again and again. This had all the earmarks of a no-win situation. If I tried to separate them, I could get one of their vicious blows to my face, and that would leave a mark. Or I could grab one and risk being accused of inappropriate action. I decided in a flash just to use my loudest, most authoritative voice to scream out, *"STOP!"* three times and hoped that someone with authority would hear. And thank goodness, it worked as a success coach along with a couple of tenured teachers quickly arrived on the scene and I just slinked away back to my quiet, final-taking classroom.

And there was evening and morning. The First Year.

Chapter 8

School's Out for Summer

One of the great perks of working for a school system is that you get summers off while still receiving checks. Technically, you don't get paid for doing nothing, they just stretch out your pay from the 184 days you are supposed to be working so it feels like you're getting paid for doing diddly. Still, it felt nice. What would have made it feel nicer if you knew going into the summer that you were definitely being brought back. Subs can't get tenure, regardless of if they are there for 8 years, as teachers do, and it's a contract job, so just before the school year ended, all the subs were herded into Principal Bowman's office and handed an official separation letter which was simply another way of saying you're fired. It helps only in the fact that you have proof of collecting unemployment if you want to go that way. I tried to circumvent the whole sweating it out during the summer thing by constantly contacting the worthless HR Manager again and again, beseeching upon her that due to my advanced age, not knowing what I'll be doing after the summer would be a major source of anxiety. She didn't exactly alleviate those fears, but she did email me, saying that *"in all likelihood,"* I would be brought back and not to worry.

Midway through the summer, the word came down that Principal Bowman would not be back, and Dr. Audrey Tingledooz would go back to being the Language Department Head. I kept emailing Worthless HR Person, and kept getting more and more ambiguous answers, ranging from you'll probably be brought back to you're not guaranteed to being brought back to finally, the new administration doesn't know you. You aren't coming back. To that last one, I let loose my pent-up snark. *"Of course. I understand. After all, they don't know me so what could I expect? If only there was a way for potential employers to know the people who are interested in working for them. What did you and Tingledooz do when you didn't know me?? Wasn't it some new-fangled invention they refer to as the interview???"*

I did some digging and found that the new people would be Principal Donald Cronnenborg, a large, bald-headed man who once worked in the prison system. He was the type of man you want to see on the deck of the Titanic. You knew he would lead you out of it and if he couldn't, you knew he did everything possible and would gladly go down with the ship to save as many others that he could. Vice Principals Sherman Granger, the athlete, drill sergeant and psychotherapist who could handle any situation and Vice Principal Conor O'boy, a totally chill, happy leprechaun that believed everything were his Lucky Charms and was totally unrufflable. They all came through the district system and probably had their own people in mind as school districts work on the friends and nepotism plan. I immediately set out to email all three over and over until I got some response. I finally heard back from VP Granger who agreed to meet me at the school. He was a young handsome, sharp-dressed black man who looked no-nonsense. I told him about my background in film and television and why I loved being a substitute teacher and absolutely wanted to come back, and that if they were truly interested, they could have me for the next 5 years as that's when I was planning on retiring, and I would love it if this position could be the coda to my career. VP Granger reacted very strongly to my pitch and told me that *"Hell yeah, we want you back."* He went on to say that it would be great if I could end up teaching in their film/TV department, but that wouldn't be up to him. The bottom line was that I broke through the wall of my-non-response-is-my-response and got back in. The bonus being that I really liked VP Granger, especially when I learned that he would oversee the subs. You could talk business with him and get a direct answer. Perfect.

When I returned to school the following September, VP Granger and Science Department Chair, Doris Burrito were waiting for me.

They told me that due to a shortage of science teachers, I would have to teach chemistry, possibly for the entire year if they can't hire an actual science teacher. Ah, chemistry and math; the courses that vexed me back when I was a high school student over 50 years ago. Still, it was obviously a compliment that they chose me over any of the other subs that were hired. It might have been due to my covering a teacher's environmental and forensic biology classes last year for over a month as she recovered from knee-replacement surgery. As she knew she would be out in advance, she prepared all the classwork by date. Unfortunately, Dr. Burrito would give me the work completely out of sync, so that I eventually ran out of work to give the students an entire week before my stint ended. I thought that wouldn't bode well for this new assignment.

The first class I had was the honors class which was a good thing. Honors and AP classes had smart, self-motivating students who did the work without much prompting, although sometimes, guidance would stick people in them who had no business of being in an honors class. That proved to be true as my old friend, Lucy, was there, so drama would be a big part of that class. There were other, notable contributors such as Liza, whom I called Q as a reference to the TV special featuring Liza Minelli called, *"Liza with a Z,"* which I changed to Q because so many Brazilian names have letters in them that aren't pronounced. Q never stopped talking, especially about herself, and often in a loud, brassy voice. She rubbed many students the wrong way, but I found her to be a hoot. She would often come behind the desk to gab with me (non-stop), but she did the work and was an A student with big plans for wealth and fame. There was that couple you didn't know whether to root for or against, Marcelo and Beatriz. Marcelo was funny; always paranoid about his grades, his relationship, everything, while Beatriz was confident about herself to a fault, that you wondered why she wasn't dating a jock instead of a low self-esteem brainiac. Genesis was a tiny thing with anxiety issues who started sitting behind my desk as she said that my presence calmed her down. Prior to working at the school, NO ONE ever said anything remotely like that and suddenly, students galore reiterated this before, unknown power I had.

Most of the other classes were much tougher. All the classes had lab tables where the knuckleheads would sit with their friends and just cause havoc all during the period, refusing to listen to the "sub," with no chemistry teaching experience, attempting to lecture them on "sig figs" (significant figures). One class that had a lot of the football jocks was the unruliest one I had and forced the "chill sub with the crazy clothes" to lose his Zen exterior and yell on more than one occasion. It was effective momentarily, but once they got over the shock of my yelling, they would go back to doing their own thing and ignore any attempt of mine to get things back on track.

It didn't help matters that Dr. Burrito refused to give me any advance notice of the lectures and material needing to be covered that day. She would ask to meet me in her office before classes to give me what I needed, and to hunt for a working copier machine to make the copies required. She was always late by at least 20 minutes, and one time, when I had the unmitigated gall to complain about wasting my time by her always being late, she snapped at me to "*shut my cakehole.*" Normally, I would never let anyone speak to me like that, but she was the department head, and technically I was her employee, and I never felt not on thin ice at the school, regarding the short shelf-life of substitute teachers, even one like me who was the one they turned to teach during a long-term assignment.

When I told her about the problems I had in the one class, she decided to come in and teach that class, regaling them with her jokes that she and her husband met while teaching chemistry a million years ago, and the fact that they were still together, meant that they had "*chemistry*" together, which brought on the type of groans you would expect from a comic performing in a strip club. She also decided to cut me off at the knees when she mentioned that due to the antics of the class, SOMEONE (and she looked at me) needed to be the adult in the room. I knew from that moment on that I would never be able to fully reel in that class. Eventually, the jock knuckleheads decided that they liked me enough to act at least in a tolerable manner, lest I be banished, and Dr. Burrito took over full time.

After a month, they did find a chemistry teacher to take over my classes. Dr. Burrito showed me her resume and I noticed that she never lasted a full year at any school she taught at. Whenever I passed one of my former chemistry students in the hallway or had them in a different class, they would tell me how horrible the new teacher was and would I please come back. Students often thought that it was up to me when I left a long-term assignment, but I felt at least slightly vindicated by their pleas for a return. Those pleas turned into guffaws when I learned that the new teacher walked out one day and quit with no notice. I wasn't put back in their classes, though. Dr. Burrito realized that they needed someone who could teach chemistry, so she reluctantly left her office and went back into the classroom. She announced her retirement from teaching that summer, after the school year. Good riddance.

One major reason I preferred long-term subbing to the daily grind of showing up in the office each morning to see which teacher's classes you would be covering that day, was cafeteria/auditorium duty. With 200 teachers on the payroll, and Covid, flu, RSV, and personal days off, often, there would be too many teachers out for subs to cover their classes. When that happened (which was practically every day), you and a couple of lucky winners would get assigned to cover periods 1 and 2 (before the lunch period) in the cafeteria and periods 3 and 4 in the auditorium. This was akin to herding cats, especially in the auditorium. First, you had to hope that someone put signage up on the appropriate rooms, letting students know where they needed to go, and then, you had to make signs for each teacher in the cafeteria and auditorium and hoped that the students knew that's where they needed to sit for us to take proper attendance. There was a duality with names in school. Many of the students had no idea what their teachers' names were, and we teachers (especially me) often struggled remembering the names of our students. It was especially embarrassing for me, as students often see the substitute teacher as a way to get frequent passes to the bathroom, their locker or the nurse, which was code for their real plan to wander the school aimlessly, using our pass similar to *The 5th Element* (1997), "multi-pass." I could write a pass for the same student again and again and STILL not remember their name unless they really pissed me off or did something to make me extraordinarily happy. We would often get students from classes we didn't expect with no advanced word from the office, or the opposite, a class wouldn't show because the teacher was present, they had a co-teacher, or a sub was assigned without us being aware. And Wi-Fi, especially in the auditorium, was always wonky and our computers couldn't get a signal. Or it did, but just when we were posting the attendance, it would blink out and we would have to try again . . . and again . . . and again. It was always dicey to have so many students congregate in one place. Plus, there was the exhausting ritual of being asked a zillion times for bathroom passes with the rule, only one male and one female allowed out at a time. When you have over 100 kids at in a huge venue, try making that rule stick. I despised the duty, but some subs preferred it as they could at least kibbitz with each other, and you didn't care if they were on their phones or not because trying to do work under those conditions was next to impossible. I always tried to get students to do their work when I was doing one-day subbing, and failing at that was when I would walk around the class to see who I might be able to engage with me, and if they balked at any course-specific discussion, I would get into good talks about other things, such as college, the work force, and how one really follows their passions, as many of them heard I did in many different fields. I felt that those discussions were often more valuable than coursework. Many students would pick my brain about relationships as many were fascinated by my two divorces and my love and devotion for my 2nd wife, or traveling, and what I thought of the different countries and cultures I encountered. It reminded me what the Dean of Freshman said at my college orientation back in 1975, *"Don't let school get in the way of your education."*

Holy moly, caf/auditorium work for me was a drag. I felt as far from being a teacher, and more as a babysitter for a nursery, as being gathered en masse brought out the worst in many of the students, and I couldn't blame them. They were being warehoused for lack of actual teachers, which wasn't the school's fault or theirs. It was just a product of the times when so many people could get sick at once.

Bathroom passes did give me carte blanche to screw with our students' minds:

Student: Hey Mister, can I have a bathroom pass?
Me: What's in it for me? Do you have any money? Tacos? Pizza?
Student: Um, no.
Me: Then why the hell should I write you a pass?
Student: Um . . . because I really must go?
Me: How do I know that? How do I know you'll even return?
Student: All my stuff is still here.
Me: Yeah, that sounds perfect. Too perfect.
Student: Mister, I really have to go.
Me: Fine. I'll write you a pass . . . THIS time.

Bathroom passes were also embarrassing, especially in my long-term assignments, when I couldn't remember the student's name, no matter how long I worked the class, or how many times I called their name in attendance or was asked for a pass.

Student: Mister, I need a pass to the bathroom.
Me: OK. What's your first name again?
Student: It's Allessandra. You ask me that every time and you always say you'll remember but you never do.
Me: Sorry. For me to get a name into my short-termmemory, you either have to do something incredibly memorable either good or bad.

Student: What do you have to do?
Me: I think you just did it.

And she did. I never forgot Allessandra's name again, and every time I saw her in the hallway, or in a classroom, I would always say, in a very loud voice, Hello Allessandra!!! Wait!!! Didn't I already mention my problems with remembering students' names, especially when writing out passes? I guess it's time for me to take the Man, TV, Camera, Pickle, Roadrunner cognitive test . . . again.

Name pronunciation was also a mine field. Most subs had the students write their names on a piece of paper and then went to X2 for attendance, but I liked the daily embarrassment of butchering their names and asking just how the hell you pronounce it. There were multiple spellings by parents who gave their children common names but made up for it with original spellings. There were names that I had a 50/50 chance of pronouncing, and I always chose the wrong one, and there were names that you had to give it the proper nuance with how you said it with the accent, Josue and Miguel were two that look easy enough but always tripped me up. Sometimes you pronounced a J as a Y and sometimes a Y had to be pronounced like a J. There were a significant number of transgender students who had their own preferred name, and while those names did show up for actual course classes, they didn't show up for the attendance roll call, which could get an icy response from the student, if a response at all when you called out their given name. The transgender students were a proud bunch and from my vantage point, didn't suffer any sort of bullying at school, but who knows what was going on at home. They really seemed to appreciate my insane fashion sense and I enjoyed having them in my classes as they were talkative in a fun way. I had some very strong tutorials from my movie theater employees on the matter as in the 9 years of ownership, I had three transgender employees and one non-binary, and they taught me a lot about pronouns and the differences between pangender, polygender, omnigender, gender fluid and gender stereotypes, which I thought I knew and learned over the decades, but my knowledge was woefully limited. The diversity at this high school went far beyond ethnicity, religion and skin color, and for that I was eternally grateful.

I was assigned to Ms. Fernandez's Spanish class for a month, and that turned out to be a mini–*West Side Story* (1961) without the gang fights choreography and singing. It was pretty much evenly divided between Brazilian students and Latino. They gravitate to one side of the classroom or the other, speaking only their native tongue, which worked out great for me as I spoke neither Spanish nor Portuguese. Both sides were loud and paid virtually no attention to me. The Brazilian kids would find music on YouTube and dance the class away. One of the boys, Wilmer, took great fun in wearing his baseball cap backwards, as American athletes did decades before and danced in front of my desk. When I would pantomime breaking him in half (he was super skinny), he would just laugh and continue to dance. Several of the Brazilian students had literally just arrived in the country that week and didn't speak a word of English, and the girls would go out of their way to try and get me to dance with them, which I felt could be a termination offense if the wrong person walked into that class at that moment. One of them was bound and determined to make me her dance partner, so I ended up typing on Google translate (which never offered up accurate translations so you never really know what you were saying), telling her that normally I would have accepted but there is a "no dancing" rule for teachers. She found that incredibly funny and gave off one of those laughs you never forget, and from that day on, whenever she saw me in the hallway, she would give me a huge hug, which I knew was also frowned upon, but to deter her would have meant shoving her which I thought could have even worse consequences.

On the Latino side, there was this boyfriend/girlfriend couple who at the beginning of every class, would try and build a fort around themselves using the desks and their fellow Latino students as walls, so they could kanoodle, I guess thinking that not being able to see them through the desks and people made then invisible in reality. I wanted to translate, "*Get a room,*" but I thought it would be lost in translation or worse, if it wasn't, would make them think that I was giving them permission. Raising my voice also had little effect, so I thought I would try something novel. I didn't take French or Spanish in high school as most everybody else did as I didn't want to follow the crowd, but more importantly, my dad thought that being a good Jew meant rejecting all things German. You don't buy a Mercedes Benz and you don't take German in high school. I thought that German, the roughest sounding of all languages, especially when spoken with a thick, Arnold Schwarzenegger accent, might get their attention, so I started shouting in German as Colonel Klink did at Colonel Hogan.

Damn, it really worked.

Not only did the dulcet sounds of shouted German phrases shut everybody up at once, but I think the fact that the teacher knew a language that they didn't, shocked them. They were used to speaking in Portuguese and Spanish, having their own private code that I and many teachers couldn't break. And they were at least trying to learn English, so they had something up on a lot of us. German scared the beJesus (beJosue?) out of them and had them looking up at me with real fear in their eyes. It didn't matter that all I was saying was, "*what time is it?*" or "*Oh, how lovely is the evening.*" I just had to say it with conviction and menace. I thought I heard one student mutter under his breath the word "s*trange,*" so I got right in his mug like a Marine drill sergeant and yelled, "*Das ist richtig!!! Ich bin Dr. Norman, du schweinhund!!*" And a supervillain was born. Or a superhero. I wasn't sure which.

Speaking of superheroes, I must give ink over to the most underappreciated, underpaid, overworked member of the educational system, the paraprofessional. When I didn't think I was being brought back to the high school (or even "demoted" to the elementary school), I applied to virtually every other school in the district and many in other districts. I was offered employment by virtually all of them, but none came within 20K of my current, high school salary. Many that didn't have any substitute teacher openings offered me the position of paraprofessional and I was shocked to learn just how little it paid in all districts, including the one I had been working in. The paras work side-by-side with the SPED teachers, offering more one-on-one with students that really require it. I had subbed many times in the SPED classes and what they do goes way over the call of duty and pays wayyyy under what it should pay under any circumstance. The classes I were in had students who were quite obviously high up on the autistic spectrum. Paras had to know exactly what their strengths and limitations were to provide instruction, mostly in life skills, but also in core classes, that could reach even those that had virtually no communication skills or ability to speak. They weren't all developmentally challenged, as many were quite intelligent, but reaching them was another story. I imagined that the para's pay came from a long, outdated idea that they were mostly women and former teachers, who were retired or close to it and just wanted to stay active and thus didn't require an actual living wage as their husbands provided that for them. It was an outrage that one could make more flipping burgers than working in a classroom with children that could sometimes be violent or could throw a fit at the drop of a hat. They knew, worked, and understood these children and provided them with the patience and understanding so that many of them could go on to live independent and productive lives. You don't age out of my high school until you're 23, and if you get to see the graduation ceremonies for the students who finally get their diploma due to the massive help and care they received from paraprofessionals – see the pride they feel and the joy their families feel for having a child with needs achieve something that they probably had doubts along the way would happen, you would know just how valuable paras are and their salaries would have to be double to just reach the level of "joke."

Many of those kids made quite the impression on me. There was Donnie, who every time he would see me in the hallways, would say, *"Why so fancy?"* And my reply was always the same. *"Because I can."* Kirk was non-verbal, but always had a grin on his face, and sometimes would find a word and say it repeatedly. He could do the work, especially math. Leonard was very autistic and would mostly play on a handheld video game, but he would respond to the teachers and paras suggestions, especially when outside. Priscilla had Down's Syndrome and would vacillate to acting quite happy, to angry, and could get physical if you weren't careful. Moses barely spoke above a whisper and would try to get all the work done, but needed a lot of attention, especially with math problems, but he never stopped trying. Ashley was a whiner and hated to do any work and preferred just to draw or color with crayons, but with enough nudging, she would complete the work assigned. Elgin was hard to watch and listen to as he was constantly picking his nose and eating it and he would make up songs about how *"everyone hates Elgin."* The paras told me that his parents were very patient, loving, and understanding, which belied his frequent bursts into song. He would constantly threaten to sue the teachers, paras, and the school if he was prevented from watching music videos on his computer. Marvin was simply a large-as-a-barge, happy, goofy kid. He was one of the students I met who aged out at 23 but did get his high school diploma and had a Cheshire Cat grin from ear to ear when handed his sheepskin. To see his smile beaming as he stood before us, upon being handed his diploma was worth staying after school and being off my usual OCD schedule. If that's how I felt, I can only imagine how he and his parents experienced it. Pure joy!!

Whatever people on the outside think of our education system, they should see what I've seen; how the teachers, paras, and administration really feel about the most vulnerable children and how hard they work for literally pennies, to enrich their lives and help them acquire the skills to do whatever it is they are able or even hope to do.

A lot of unsung school staff had and continue to be a great help to me. As I show up so ridiculously early at school, to my being allergic to starting my day in traffic and ever being late, and the fact that I go to bed insanely early, wake up maddingly earlier and use the time at school as my prep time for all the classes I have had to fake it until I made it and really teach, none of it was possible without the custodial, cafeteria and culinary staff letting me in well before 6 AM.

Chapter 9

I Am Nailed to the Hull[3]

OK, I was obviously never nailed to a hull. That line was from the first season of *Saturday Night Live's* parody of a Dickens novel, David Copperfield. *The Adventures of Miles Cowperthwaite* was a supposed table reading of the unearthed Dickens novel with *Monty Python's Flying Circus* member and guest host, Michael Palin, as the eponymous character whose wretched, painful and degrading existence that ended on a pirate ship, The Raging Queen was brought to life. At times, I did think that my life was an SNL parody because who becomes a substitute teacher in their 60's *after* Covid, with school shootings being a semi-regular, American institution? My schedule had been so heavily skewed towards early morning and it was getting to me, especially as my job duties at school continued to increase with all the long-term subbing I was doing, which I was ecstatic that they thought of me for those assignments. The flip side to that was how much of a major leap up in responsibilities it became. I'd get home before 4PM, eat and be in bed by 5. Then, I'd be up by 9:30PM, and do 1000 sit ups, 6 minutes with a shake weight, 100 reps with a rubber band, a bunch of push-ups, and then I'd hit the fitness room for 30 minutes on an elliptical, and 30 minutes of weight training. I'd head back and have breakfast before midnight and then out for a 2-mile walk. I'd do all that before the freaking next day rolled over. I'd meditate for 3 hours, shower, and then be on the road at 4:30AM for the 30-mile drive. The only positive thing that schedule does is it gives me finger-wagging privileges towards anyone that complained about how rough or long their day was. Geez, I may as well break out the nipple-pinching clothespins (another *Myles Cowperthwaite* reference).

---

3   Saturday Night Live (1975)

Eating breakfast so early, I took every opportunity to eat lunch equally early, that I made all weeks' worth of lunches on Sunday and would pack in my *I Love Lucy* lunchbox. If I had advisory or intervention off, which began at 9:25AM, that's when I ate lunch, explaining the oddness to coworkers that breakfast for me was before midnight the night before. If I was subbing on the 5th floor, I would take my lunch at the teacher's break room off the library which had the Comfy Chair, as long as I'm referencing *Monty Python*, and as someone who is licensed in World History, I AM expecting the Spanish Inquisition.

Li had been ghosting me since the YOU DON'T NEED TO FUCKING KNOW ARGUMENT with Schmucky McSchmuckface (first referenced as Franco, before "the Argument). That made sense as Li and Schmucky had known each other for years and he was also a card-carrying misogynist like Yeehaw. In fact, Schmucky was a big admirer of Yeehaw and had encouraged and supported him in his romantic entanglement with Li. It didn't matter as I had made a new friend. Freja Terrific (her last name, pronounced phonetically is Tur-Eef-Eetch," as no names at this high school were pronounced as they were spelled), was a 22-year-old sub from Bosnia whom I had gotten to know when we were both scheduled in the caf/auditorium for a few days one week. She was endlessly entertaining as she told me about her family and her wacky way of living her life. She described her parents as being in a constant state of endless divorce, which was par for the course in Bosnia, as true happiness was never really expected, and misery was often seen as a status symbol. She loved her dad, whose 20 years in the US gained him just enough English to navigate his job as an airport shuttle driver, and the two of them loved dressing in identical outfits up to and including her adulthood which flummoxed her mom who only wished for a son-in-law and grandchildren from Freja in order to be considered successful. She was the Margaret Dumont to their Groucho and Harpo. Her nickname for her older sister was "Dumbass Ho," and she declared that her rules for getting married or having any kind of long-term relationship, was her partner had to "wash their chicken and meat." I wasn't exactly sure if she meant that as meal preparation or, you know, Bosnia farm animals, and I never asked for clarification, being somewhat apprehensive of the answer. Her daily rants included the constant butchering of her last name by all who attempted it; that American television, especially reality shows like all the Housewives shows weren't her guilty pleasure, but rather her pure, unadulterated art and her confusion as to why I refused to partake was palpable. We finally found common ground when she convinced me to watch all the episodes of *Avatar: The Last Airbender* (2024), which we did in the 5th floor teacher's lounge whenever our prep periods lined up. It was fun watching her tear up when an animated, 6-legged, flying water buffalo was thought to be dying, and she was amazed at my knowledge of good writing that allowed me to predict where scenes were going to go even though the episodes were far from being predictable.

Freja had anxieties on top of her anxieties and was even more cynical than I, again, something that I thought must have been produced by being born in a war-torn region that the US had a huge hand in screwing up. She was a lot of fun to talk to and loved to prattle on about all the "T" (or is it spelled "tea?") that she couldn't wait to share with me. She also was, admittedly, the laziest person on the planet which is why she refused to hang out with me outside of school as that would either mean her driving distance to where I live, or my meeting her parents, or us having to travel to go somewhere else and do something. We were school chums, and our personalities seemed to mesh, and it was always a nice feeling when she saw me unexpectedly in the hallways or near her classroom and see her smile.

The other subs brought in for my second year were mostly people that came up through the system and were both students and had worked with Vice Principal Granger. They were jocks and coaches and assistant coaches for the football, basketball, and baseball teams, some of whom played Division 1 and even had a taste of pro ball, albeit a Mexican football league. They weren't interested in going on to become teachers, as sports were their thing. They were good dudes and were great to work with in the caf/ auditorium as they had relationships with the jocks/knuckleheads of the school and were obviously fantastic when it came to discipline. I got along with all of them and enjoyed talking about sports as they also respected my knowledge of athletes from yesteryear, and they also enjoyed my Forrest Gumpian stories of the life I had led. Two subs did have their sights on a career in academia. One was from Haiti and an active, amateur fighter. He was a helluva guy and we really got along well, and whatever path he chose going forward, I have no doubt that he will achieve. The other was a tiny beauty whose name fit her perfectly, Serena Swan. She saw herself going into guidance and she's another whose success is guaranteed.

And there was evening and morning; The Second Day.

Chapter 10

Hippopotamus Leg Theorem

It's really called the Hypotenuse Leg Theorem, but it might as well be hippopotamus with my understanding of it. They have me teaching Geometry (two mainstream and two honors) and Algebra II (both honors), and my memory of those classes from 50 years ago, which were never my best subjects then, well, they might as well be hieroglyphics in an ancient, Egyptian cave or on the side of a Sphinx for as much as I understand it. It harkens back to an old, Groucho Marx quote:

Why, it's simple. A four-year old child can understand it.
Hey Shorty, go round up a four-year old child. I can't make heads or tails of this thing.

My fourth, long-term gig of the year; three in a row due to maternity and paternity leave, but this is a spider hole I must crawl in unarmed. Math is a core subject which means the students really must pass them and a state math test to graduate. Due to how overcrowded the school is, the guidance counselors put the squeeze on teachers to pass the students regardless of grade to make room for the next batch coming up from middle school. On the one hand, their refrain to the teachers is *"Rigor! Rigor! Rigor!"* They drill this into our heads, regarding how the students need to be taught, making sure they understand the basics of each course, and the ones that are in the honors sections, should have been able to handle the more difficult work. The reality was that many of the students knew there were more openings in the honors classes and were able to finagle their guidance counselors to allow a bunch of their friends to all be in class together, often, the knuckleheads who would rather disrupt the class then buckle down and do the work, and then rent their garments when they see their F grades followed by the student begging rituals or pleading to get an "I" for incomplete. That granted them a stay of execution for two more weeks to get their incomplete work in and you'll be lucky to see them in class again. I felt somewhat relieved to have a co-teacher, Les Arrow, for two of the classes on A days, the classes that contain most of the aforementioned knuckleheads, and he's a Bonafide math teacher. I'm OK with geometry as it's mostly spatial relationships which appeal to the filmmaker in me, but Algebra II is a lost cause. Just the mention of quadratic equations, factoring and imaginary numbers can put me in a semi-catatonic state. For the classes that Les isn't there with me for algebra, I mostly just project the lesson on a slide show where the answers to each practice equation appear piece by piece as I hit the down button, and I hope that the class understands exactly how it got to the final answer. I asked the department head to start showing up for some of the algebra classes and he agreed. Turns out he only took the Department head job to make sure he isn't fired as he once worked under one that just had it in for him. He really missed teaching and it showed the first time I saw him work. He knows the gibberish, loves it and can connect to the students, even those who, like me, are math resistant. For the classes that he takes over and the ones with Les, I don't feel like I'm standing in front of the class in pink, banana hammock underwear trying to sputter out a lucid lecture on polynomials. I did achieve a crowning success in one my honors Geometry classes. I have two honors geometry classes back-to-back on B days. The first class is generally catatonic or lobotomized, I can't tell the difference. I can never get them to participate, talk or even grunt as I'm going through a slide-show presentation on parallelograms or some other fascinating, geometric concept and just need to know if I can proceed to the next slide. The second class is much livelier, due to a group of female friends who get A+s on virtually everything but treat each class as if they're having a sleepover. They push their tables together, and constantly talk, share TikTok videos, discuss boys or other, important topics of the day and basically see me as an amusing pet. I tried something with the same, mind-numbing, parallelogram lecture that failed miserably in the previous class. I called one of the pajama party leaders, a very tall, dancing, girl named Ludmila, to come up and show the class how to solve the problem on the board, or the case of the Missing Angle. She proceeded to give a thorough, and correct lecture as to the math, needed to solve for "X," drawing on the projected slide in handwriting you could read as opposed to my illegible scrawl, and often shushing her fellow partners-in-crime when they began their usual talking amongst themselves instead of paying attention. Sisters Iracema and Valderine, who will probably keep talking even in a coma, immediately clammed up, followed by Lais, Elolisa and Talita. Ludmila looked at me and said, *"Wow. How do you do this every day?"* I just smiled, elated with the idea that at least this class at this moment, seemed to get it. I just let Ludmila go through the rest of the slides and all the problems, and the class joined in with others coming to the board to show the math needed to solve a particular problem. I was jubilant. My hope that the students could be the ones to really teach each other and participate in class where it was fun but also extremely helpful to the many other students who often struggled with remembering if they need to use the Pythagorean or Interior Angles Theorem and then what number do you choose to get rid of other numbers and isolate X. Having fellow students willfully and energetically teach them how to do it so they wrote it down and understood, gave me the Dopamine high I imagined my students got as they noodled with their phones during my sleep-inducing droning.

Midterms were another story. The algebra classes had an online test that obviously ventured into areas not totally covered by my classes. Once submitted, it gave you your score, and several of the A students started crying, thinking their GPAs were now shot to hell, thus kissing off their chances of an ivy league education, or at least something Like Tufts University or NYU. I was able to see their scores on my computer and the highest scores were in the low 80s, not a single natural A from anyone, and many of the students were math savants. I assured them that there would be partial credits assigned for getting some of the equations correct and that the tests would be graded on a curve. The sight of formerly smiling, laughing and happy kids thinking that their lives just got flushed and possibly pointing a finger at their teacher-of-record as the reason was unsettling, to say the least. They knew that I always advocated for them in any way I could by extending deadlines on classwork and homework and removing the points penalties for completing those online assignments late. I couldn't shake the feeling that their failure was really MY failure, even though I knew that I did the best I could. I studied more than most of them to try and learn the curriculum but learning for yourself and teaching it are two totally different skill sets, one most people should understand when they accuse teachers of having an easy, part-time job. I get it while a teacher "only" works 184 days in a school year. That number still produces burnout quickly, so extending class time, as some outsiders suggest, would only create a larger black hole regarding the current teacher shortage by accelerating burnout. You stare at the school calendar and mentally mark off the long weekends and week-long breaks so you can pace yourself. It's like driving cross country and you must look at the signs that tell you how many miles to the next town rather than think about the actual number of miles you must go before reaching your much further destination, or you'll go mad.

I'm not going mad (too late), but my paranoia burns bright. I keep imagining that the teacher who is out, comes back, sees how poorly her students did under my tutelage and puts all the blame on my incompetence, even though we talked prior to her leave, and she understood my lack of math credentials and appreciated my willingness to go out there each day for months and give it the ole high school try. This is where the knuckleheads helped me. I was able to get them to do their work prior to midterms to get most of their grades into the passing level. They tried their usual shenanigans during the midterm tests; asking for passes to the bathroom or nurse and I kept busting them taking walks, with their cell phones on them; a huge no-no as all phones had to be on my desk during quizzes and tests. I enjoyed the cat-and-mouse games where the house always won as none of them were the con men they believed themselves to be. The looks on their faces when I told them I knew where they really were and what they were doing relegated them to stuttering, gurgling messes while I played whack-a-mole with their litany of excuses. There was always the implied wink as they knew that I basically liked them, despite their need for attention or perhaps because of it. Most of them did get the assignments done, proving to both me and them that they weren't the dimbulbs most people thought, probably including themselves. I always knew that cheating on online assignments was possible, nay probable, but I felt that they had to learn a little bit by osmosis just being exposed to the work. I encouraged their rebellious spirits but hoped to challenge and channel it in areas where pushing the envelope was a necessary part of being young and to not blindly accept authority, even mine, if they felt it unjust. They never cease to amaze. After one Honors Algebra II math test, I decided to look at the logs of a few of the knuckleheads in that class and something stood out. One of the K-heads' computer test indicated that six of the questions were answered in under ten seconds. That seemed implausible as you had to work out the math on scratch paper before you had even a modicum of a chance of picking the correct option for the answer. He got 7 out of 10 correct for the entire test, as did his other partners in crime, all except for one who got a 2. I remembered one of them asking for a pass to the bathroom, which I allowed as it was a short test, and I couldn't think of any way for him or anyone to cheat. They didn't have their phones and even if they did, it wasn't The Weakest Link where you could phone a friend. They did something though, which was semi-confirmed when the student asked me during the next class if he could see his test and see which answers he missed. He had a smirk on his face the whole time, but I couldn't think of a single way that he could have received answers for an online test while at the bathroom or anywhere, yet the similar scores and the lightning-quick answering of several questions was baffling. The kid got me. He and his buddy-buds got me. I don't know how but they did. I'll be ready for them . . . next time.

I have no illusions or delusions of the long-term impact of my pleadings and exhortations of the students to do their work, but the hope that part of the life lesson could stick with some of them. What I lacked in math skills I made up with experience and navigating a plethora of bullshit that the labyrinth of life presents. I often thanked my students for what they gave me; the possibilities to learn and present material that I had long since forgotten, which can only hold off dementia at least until I retire, hopefully in three years. I look ahead fondly to my apartment in Kuala Lumpur that will cost a fraction of what rents are in the US, heading out to the street food vendors to dine on Masak Lemak, Asam Pedas or Kari Ikan followed by a nice dip in the apartment complex's indoor pool and ending in a massage. I only need to maintain enough brain cells to keep that lifestyle going, and being forced fed a diet of biology, math and whatever subject lurks in my future should guarantee me that *Midnight Cowboy* (1969) dreamscape.

While I bask in Southeast Asian luxury, I'm sure that my mind, as a film guy, would reflect on all the high school movies I've seen to see how my experience ranked. Movies such as *Blackboard Jungle* (1955), *To Sir with Love* (1967), *Rebel Without a Cause* (1955), *Lean On Me* (1989) and *The Principal* (1987) went with the teens as dangerous or at least uncouth punks and there are some of that where I am, but nothing so dramatic. Of course, my Skittles Collection tends to diffuse that element when they see me. Movies that try to show teenage archetypes like *The Breakfast Club* (1985), *Dazed and Confused* (1993), *American Graffiti* (1973) and *Mean Girls* (2004) feel more suburban, than my school does and while they are some of my personal favorites in the genre, I don't see the representation, but they did take place in the suburbs of Chicago,

Texas, San Francisco and LA again. I tried to do research before starting my first day and to that end, I found a streaming show placed in a modern high school called *One of Us is Lying* (2024) but was just a retelling of *The Breakfast Club* (1985) with the Princess, Brain, Jock, Basket Case and Criminal all the stars except now they're all psychopaths with mad social media skills. It wasn't helpful. *Bring It On* (2000) could have worked had all the cheerleaders spoken Spanish and Portuguese. Fair enough. I guess I'm left with parsing this entire experience myself because all experience is personal unless I party with Mayans and partake of their Amanita muscaria and Sinicuichi and eat a live lizard and enjoy a communal experience that hopefully, doesn't resemble Edvard's Munch's painting, *The Scream*.

Chapter 11

Monday the Grateful Substitute Teacher Froze His Ass Off

If you grew up Jewish in Massachusetts during the 60's as I did, your parents probably had the series of books by author Harry Kellerman with titles such as, *Friday the Rabbi Slept Late* (1964) or *Wednesday the Rabbi Got Wet* (1976). Yes, he had a title for every day of the week and when he ran out of those, they became more non-specific, such as *Someday the Rabbi Will Leave* (1987). I bring this up only because during my morning, 30-mile drive to school, which took about 40 minutes, and often, during my return drive home, which took 60 - 90 minutes, depending upon the stupidity of the drivers that day, I sometimes mused about titles featuring me in them, regarding that day's personal experience or obsession. My early entry into the school building (I would arrive around 5:10AM), depended on a myriad of circumstances and people. I parked right outside the 4th floor doors so when school was done, I could make a beeline for my car and get out of Dodge before the shiny, metal boxes began their sojourn home. Every minute I delayed added 20 minutes to the drive home. Some days, I would be able to access the building at those 4th floor doors because the gym was right there and many days, with no perceivable pattern I ever decoded, some staff members would arrive early to either play basketball or work out in the weight room. They got in thanks to Ethan, a science teacher with 20 years of service and he had a key. He had given out his phone number to select people and they would call him and he would arrive to let them in as he was in the building even earlier than that so he could work out and get all of his anger and frustrations out before the great unwashed student population arrived at 7:30AM.

Ethan was a righteous dude but I sensed a bubbling volcano underneath so I never asked for his number, and was just happy that on some days, I could get in early and find the one, working printer to get out that day's assignment packet before all the other teachers arrived and the queue for each printer resembled a ride at Disneyworld which then assumed that the ride was still operational when you finally got to the front of the line.

On unlucky days, I would walk about a quarter mile down the hill to the school's front doors where a smattering of people had ID badges that opened the doors earlier than my ID did. There was Frank, the head of the Custodian Department, who was a little like Carl, the janitor from *The Breakfast Club* (1985), only much crazier. Frank was a lifer and I heard that at one point, he loved his job and the kids, but that certainly wasn't the case anymore. On the days when he was my access, he never said hi or any greeting that could be considered even semi-normal. He would just start ranting about how stupid everyone was and how he hated days when he had to shovel the stairs so "Juan" wouldn't have to get his feet wet in the snow or slip on the ice or some other tragedy Frank obviously wished upon poor Juan. Other days, he would be staring up at the sky, frozen until I said something, and his response would be something like, "*Watching for the aliens. I heard this is the day they might be coming.*" Teachers and administrators are obviously not the only school staff members that burn out. Frank often obsessed over the orange cones that were out near the school trucks that were parked near the front, and he would move them all a fraction of an inch in one direction or the other. I wondered if he did that just to delay opening the door for me, but I dared not ask or say anything to him that might cause whatever was burning in his soul to escape in my direction.

Tippy worked in the cafeteria and his badge became operational at 6:45AM. To Tippy, everything was a conspiracy theory so it was best not to say anything that could lead down a dark road as there would be no turning back. Everyone was in on everything, so even a sneeze would lead him into talking about diseases, vaccines, 9-11, Kennedy, Taylor Swift, Hollow Earth, Flat Earth, Triangle Earth, Eartha Kitt, Kit Kat Bars, Bar Mitzvahs etc. Tippy was cocooned in paranoid fantasies designed to confuse and amuse himself because I didn't want to get into any of them. Shockingly, he was recently fired.

Carey was in the culinary department, a big bear of a man who rarely smiled but talking with students about him, he was adored. He would arrive, full steam ahead to the doors, and I learned to keep chit chat to a minimum, at least at that hour. If I ran into him during the day, he would thaw out and be friendlier, so I just took it that he wasn't much of a morning person and was just grateful when he was on the scene before Frank or Tippy. Finally, there was Shirley, the Administrative Assistant to the Principal and Vice Principals. Shirley was another one who spent most of her life in the school district, but far from being burned out, talking to Shirley was like receiving a verbal hug. She was so happy and fun and caring, and she would do anything for the staff and kids. Her desk housed a myriad of glass canisters, filled with candy for all to reach in to make their day sweeter. She knew everyone and everyone knew her, and you wouldn't hear a negative trait about her from anyone. If you wanted your day to start off right, you hoped that Shirley was your first encounter.

Finally, there was Pip, another cafeteria worker along with his two lady accomplices, Alice and Ida. Pip would arrive first and then wait for Alice and Ida who carpooled. Pip was married to Claudia, a paraprofessional I met early in my first year, and we discovered that my dad delivered her and virtually her entire family. Pip, Alice and Ida would walk towards me and the front door where Pip's badge would work at 6:00AM, and Pip would always have a smart remark about whatever color pants I was wearing that day. If they were green, it would be, *"Look, it's Mr. Green Jeans,"* a nod to a character on the 60's kid's show, *Captain Kangaroo*. My orange pants elicited the pun, *"Orange you glad I'm here now?"* while purple brought out,

"*It's the Flying Purple People Eater*," or, "*Hey, it's Barney.*" I never responded as I was simply glad to see Pip and his crew because if they were letting me in, it meant that I was standing outside for at least 30 minutes. It could be 30 minutes in freezing cold, or rain, snow, locusts or boils, and it was those moments that my mind would drift off and think about how it was that I got there, and what I was doing and thought about all those Harry Kellerman Rabbi books, creating new titles describing me and whatever situation struck my fancy. I knew that at some point, I would be sitting in front of my computer, allowing my stream of consciousness to flow and get this experience down. It's changed me, right down to my DNA, and I'm sure Tippy would have some words about that.

Chapter 12

Paper Teacher

I often felt like George Plimpton, the writer and sports journalist who embarked on a Walter Mitty type life by attempting to participate in pro sports endeavors such as boxing, football, baseball and hockey and then writing about the experience in Sports Illustrated. His attempt at pro football was the source for his 1966 book, *Paper Lion* that became a feature film in 1968. He wasn't accepted by the team's actual players who immediately saw that he lacked any kind of athletic ability, and they hazed him mercilessly. In practice, he initially went to the wrong player to put his hands under center, lost yardage on the only plays they allowed him to call, and he even tripped over his own feet and sacked himself when dropping back to pass. I know the feeling.

Every day during my geometry, algebra assignment I stand up in front of the class feeling like a total fraud for even attempting to teach something that I don't grasp with the fluidity necessary to convey how to do it to a room full of bored teenagers. Many of them stay on their phones or just listen to music with their ear buds; walk around the room and interact with their friends as if they are in the basement of their homes, indifferent to my droning on and on about isosceles trapezoids or doing the math to find how many bags of sod you need to cover a huge lawn. I'm naked, vulnerable and exposed. It's not exactly a new feeling for me. I attempted stand-up comedy when I was 25, getting up at Open Mic night at the Comedy Club in Denver, once having to follow rising comic Rosanne Barr who totally killed it that night. It goes back to our basic needs to be approved and everybody, at some point, becomes our parents. You reveal all your flaws and neuroses when you put yourself out there like that.

I have had a reoccurring nightmare for decades. I'm back in college, but I'm always my current age. I know that I haven't done whatever work was needed, be it reading chapters, writing a paper or studying for a test. To complicate matters, I'm wandering around campus, having totally forgotten where the building with my class is located or anything that clues me in to where I am. I have read up on this dream and consulted therapists when I had them and the books and psychologists seem to agree that dreams where you are back at school, but totally unprepared are a sign that you are suffering from Imposter Syndrome. When Harry Potter was informed that he was a wizard, he recoiled at the possibility, insisting that it must have been a mistake. He just knew that he couldn't be magical.

Perhaps that was why I donned the "Skittles" look, to hide the fact that I didn't belong there and who was I to think for one second that I could impart knowledge and wisdom to children looking up at me, hoping to get a magic elixir of facts that would make everything all right in their hardscrabble lives. Of course, they retreat behind the safety and comfort of their phones. They don't see me as their teacher, but a clown attempting to be both a ventriloquist and sleight-of-hand expert. It's all in the misdirection.

You can't let those thoughts permeate or else you'll be completely paralyzed. You must become the *Saturday Night Live* character, Stuart Smalley and look in the mirror and repeat your affirmation, *"I'm good enough. I'm smart enough. And gosh darn it, these kids like me."* After all, the administration has complete faith in you, but you often wonder if it's just that you're the best option they have and not based on your talent. I remind myself that I've been through this movie before. Nobody taught me how to establish and run an international film festival. You received no training about how to be an Information Manager at Olympic Games venues and there was no tutorial regarding creating, writing and producing a syndicated radio show. The biggest difference between those events and substitute teaching is that failing the prior mostly impacted me, while screwing up this gig can have an enormous, domino effect on children; children who are depending on you to help them develop their critical thinking and social skills, even if they don't understand that's the real purpose of high school.

George Plimpton failed miserably at every sport he attempted because of course he did. Pro athletes are elite. Even the bench players who rarely see any action are still in the top percentile of people in their respective sport. He went out there, screwed it up and wrote fascinating articles about the heightened sense of the experience he received just from the attempt. He held his head up high, knowing that all the embarrassments were short-lived and that it was all a part of his true calling, writing, and in that he triumphed.

Writing this book isn't the same thing, not by a long shot. Regardless of potential sales, this can't be the achievement. It must be the ability to get a large percentage of the children in my charge to grasp the material and not lose ground until their *real* teacher gets back. I'm not a fake. I can't be. If all goes according to plan, I'll be doing this for three more years.

Chapter 13

Buenos Noches y Buena Suerte. Boa Noite e Boa Sorte. Bòn Nwit ak Bon Chans. Bonne Nuit et Bonne Chance

They were lying in wait for me.

After yet another summer when I didn't hear back from the district if I would be brought back or not, even though the worthless HR Manager, Tracy Phipp was no longer there, and neither was VP Granger who fled south to warmer climes; my initial support system and main reason I was back for a second year. He was replaced by Allen Impala, who looked like a Mini Cronnenborg, but I soon discovered that he was a good dude and someone you could do business and not be in constant fear of your job. Some things didn't change and it still wasn't until the end of August that I got the new contract letter. Still, I didn't sweat it quite as badly as I did the previous two summers. I never even applied for any other jobs or even looked. I felt that I proved myself as a building asset, especially as I was constantly being asked to do long-term assignments and teach various courses. Plus, I was the co-winner of "Best Dressed Teacher," although my co-winner was what the gals from the movie *Clueless* (1995) would have referred to as a Baldwin; all muscles, man-bun (since shorn) and sleeve tattoos, and nothing that could be called any type of taste in clothing. OK, that's not fair. He did have a great shoe game. Of course, there was nothing about my wardrobe that screamed taste; it just screamed. I was a walking, LSD flashback, not that any of the students would understand that, as vaping was their drug of choice, at least at school, where their efforts would be Big Brothered due to the vape monitors installed in the bathrooms over the summer, although they discovered ways to beat the monitors, leaving security baffled as just the flip they did it. I felt confident of my value, and that confidence played out when I was immediately met in the front office mere seconds after walking in on the first school day for faculty and staff. Beano Burgermeister, the newly promoted Science Department Chair for the since-retired Doris Burrito, and Tori McKnight, the Head of the English Language Learning (ELL) Department swooped down on me, all smiles pleading looks welcomed me with open arms, and a proposition. With the exodus of so many people in the math and science departments, and a lack of interested candidates willing to fill those positions, they wanted me to be the Sheltered Biology teacher for as long as it took before they could hire someone with an actual biology background, which they quickly said could take a year or more. I had subbed for Beano's classes many times the previous year as he was out sick a lot, and I knew Tori from several conversations we had when I was subbing in a class across from hers. The only thing I really knew about Beano was that his students weren't fans. They had told me that he mostly has them watch videos and that he just wasn't very personable. Tori, I really liked it. She was incredibly friendly and at one point during the previous school year, she told me in front of another faculty member that I was one of the nicest guys in school; a compliment that rarely was thrown in my direction. Maybe she was just pre-buttering me up for something that she knew was inevitable. I knew that my value as a long-term sub, someone that was willing and able to go in the classroom and attempt to teach a subject that wasn't in my wheelhouse, which was basically every subject that wasn't history, English, film, television, pop culture or, in a pinch, psychology. Biology was something I hadn't studied since I was in high school, some 50 years ago, and sheltered meant that the students spoke little to no English, meaning they would need to be reached in ways that preclude my being able to speak Spanish, Portuguese, Haitian Creole, and French. I was promised to receive massive support from both departments, but there was no question about my accepting this *Mission Impossible* (1966). It's what I did and what I hoped my reputation would do for me. Both also said that they had spoken with the administration and my name was the only one that came up. Whether that was the truth or not, didn't matter. The fact that they felt the need to give me the hard sell told me how desperate they were and how much this could really make my stock increase. If I was not only able to teach these classes but succeed at doing it, I wouldn't have another summer of flop sweats again.

Of course, there was a catch. Well, maybe not so much a catch as a caveat. The Department of Elementary and Secondary Education (DESE), which oversaw licensure and education standards in the state, had chosen a company called Open Science Education (OpenSciEd) to teach biology; a core course of which students must not only pass the course curriculum, but also the MCAS (Massachusetts Comprehensive Assessment System) in order to graduate from high school. There was a lot of pushbacks throughout the state, whether the tests were fair and unbiased and were good metrics of which to judge a student's proficiency in math, science and English, and there was a petition going around to get the MCAS tests banished. Schools like mine were under a lot of pressure to get the MCAS scores up as they had been on a downward curve, which should have been expected due the number of students we had from Central and South America, not to mention Haiti, Vietnam and other countries, then factor in cell phone distractions and the pause Covid created in all school systems. This meant that I was going to be teaching a curriculum that none of the other biology teachers had taught or even saw before. In many ways, I might have been better off than the actual bio teachers as I had no methods to unlearn.

OpenSciEd was geared towards having students acting like scientists. They were to be broken up into small groups often to make various observations on what we were studying, as questions about them and then answer them amongst themselves, just as the scientific community does in real life. That would be great if students had any introduction to those methods in elementary and middle school. As it was, especially post pandemic, they had very little interest in interacting with anybody at all except their phones. I would come into a classroom of as few as 10 people that I was subbing for and say, "*good morning*," only to be greeted by total silence and not even see a single head tilt up.

I met with Tori, and her ESL coworker, Melissa, to discuss my approach to teaching a course of which I was unfamiliar to students whom we could not effectively communicate with in English. She told me that you had to be very animated and use your entire body to convey your message. She explained that a lot of the curriculum was based on "Turn and talk" and so you should be over-the-top in your movements and facial expressions to get that across. I smiled and said that's right in my wheelhouse as I am basically a cartoon character, like the Road Runner. She said that she would be with me for my first class the next day in order to demonstrate how to teach ESL.

I went over some of the OpenSciEd course on Canvas, a teaching app that most students were familiar with regarding getting their lessons, reading assignments and quizzes. The biology module was based on environmental biology, with a lot of it stemming from the 30 by 30 initiative, which proposed to protect 30% of lands and waters by 2030 and the reasons that humans engage in conservation. The module would go over four different ecosystems; a large lake in the Great Lakes; a rainforest/river system in Washington State; a desert system in Arizona, and the Everglades in Florida. It would go into these ecosystems with their interactions with the 4 components; humans, plants, animals and land/water, and then go into food webs and food chains. This all seemed well and good, but I thought that the MCAS was mostly based on molecular biology, and if the entire idea was to teach students for the test, I wasn't sure how this would fit, especially taught by a non-biology teacher, working with non-English-speaking students.

My first class of the new school year was in a large room with a huge beam on one side, partitioning the class by two thirds. After taking attendance, it was easy to surmise that the class had already separated themselves by language, with all the Portuguese-speaking Brazilians grouped together, the Spanish-speaking students in another section, and the lone Haitian sitting by himself in a corner. Tori and I started lecturing, with me leading off and she, as she said, going into exaggerated motions when it came time for the first "turn and talk." Tori, being young, attractive and very experienced with these kids, was able to cajole at least some of them into participating and asking questions they had based on what we were teaching. We were working a lot on vocabulary, which meant writing the words down, and going over it in all three languages and then having the class repeat the words three times. For "turn and talk," they were supposed to use a word in a sentence, spoken in English. It was another thing they had to get used to, speaking in class in English, something even students born in the US felt uneasy doing, either due to a lack of confidence in their abilities, or again, having their neural pathways totally rewired by the dopamine shots their phones gave them. It was hard not to get motivated when you had Tori jumping all over the place like a frog, and me, the psychedelic reaction sub right behind her. I felt a little better about how this all might go down, but I was still unsure and uneasy how it would work solo. 85 total minutes, the time for period one and intervention, before we get to period two, would be all the time I would get to find out.

The next class was in a room known as The Great Room, as it wasn't intended to be a classroom. The ceiling was 5 stories up and it was so cavernous as to be intimidating. Classrooms on upper floors could peer down into the classroom and it echoed as if you were standing in the middle of Grand Central Station. This was a mainstream bio class and not sheltered, but I thought that it might be harder to get students to talk in that environment. At least there would be less of a language barrier.

The last class of the day was oriented with all the chairs set together in small groups, facing each other, which I thought might facilitate working together, but I soon discovered that one of the students had basically skipped school every single day the previous year and still somehow got promoted to high school. She and her friend wouldn't keep quiet as they just discussed whatever it was on their phones, and once I directed my speech toward them, the School Skipper would just keep talking at me, not waiting for responses and with a huge attitude. I knew that this class might be the most challenging of all. My first class the next day was also sheltered, and it was a reasonable-sized classroom with much fewer students, and they quickly demonstrated that they would be the easiest group to deal with and have them do what is asked of them without either ignoring me or backtalk in whatever language they felt comfortable in. I tested their resolve right out of the gate by seeing if I could get them to do some breathing exercises at the beginning of class. They all stood when asked and did the exercises. At least one of my sheltered classes looked like it could be smooth sailing and something to look forward to assuming that the other classes would take as much out of me as it appeared from the first day.

The other classes were proving to be more problematic. The first class with the large pillar had all sorts of obstacles. Boulou, the student from Haiti, was incredibly unresponsive, no matter how much I translated what I was teaching and what I was translating for him into Haitian Creole, until I discovered that he spoke Spanish. I can only imagine his frustration when his teacher, who spoke in an unrecognizable language was translating into yet another bunch of gibberish to him. Most of the Brazilian boys huddled together to watch soccer videos, and then I discovered that a couple of them couldn't really read Portuguese, making my Google Translate attempts worthless. I talked to Tori about it all and she told me that many of them had come from immigration camps from all over the world and who knew what kind of abuse they might have suffered, which led to trauma and hampered all learning. I hypothesized that Boulou reacted much better to Tori than me probably due to trauma from men, and I was a large man at that. I knew that it would take more patience, understanding, and new methods to try and break through to the students most needing it, while not neglecting the students who were making real attempts at improving their English so that they could do the classwork and just survive in this country that supposedly held so much promise for them.

Meanwhile, I still found that School Skipper was problematic. It didn't help that her friend, sitting next to her in the class, cared more about working on her face, using her cell phone as a mirror than participating or completing any classwork. The class was full of all sorts of rebellious youth, having tantrums and standing firmly on their right to resist doing any kind of classwork. School Skipper concerned me the most. I finally looked at her IEP and it was as long as a CVS receipt, with all sorts of traumas and issues. The one that stood out was "Tourette's Syndrome." In her case, it didn't present as sudden outbursts of "Fuck! Shit! Cock!" Perhaps her intransigence and constant talking was her form of outburst. I decided to take a different tack and try to do all kinds of positive reinforcement. The next class, where I gave them a short, written assignment to do and she refused, I told her to write anything, even Mary had a Little Lamb. And that's exactly what she wrote, and I smiled and told her that I would give her a high grade for it as she did write something, and it was what I asked her to write. Each class, I would see if I could find some way to positively reinforce a behavior and it seemed to be working. She seemed to be smiling more at our interactions and getting her to at least some attempt at classwork was no longer like pulling teeth.

I knew that things were really going well with School Skipper on the night of the parent/teacher conference. Freja and I were heading to a restaurant to have dinner before the conference started, when I saw School Skipper riding in a car with whom I presumed was her dad. She started calling out to me from the car and signaled me to come over to say hi. As I ambled close to the car's passenger side to say hi, her dad leaned over and gave me a big smile, and said, *"Hi, Mr. Norman. I've heard so much about you and I just wanted to say hello and I'll be coming up to your classroom to visit."* That was like hearing the Jupiter Symphony for the first time. It was everything a teacher, let alone the ultimate temp, could wish to hear. I smiled back and told him that it was my pleasure to meet him and how much I liked having his daughter in my class. My class. That's what it was. They might eventually hire someone to replace me (and a month later, they did), but until then, this was my class, with my students learning whatever it was I was tasked to teach them and maybe, just maybe, a wee bit more.

As mentioned, teaching sheltered biology came to a halt when the school did find someone to replace me; a recent, 22-year-old, college graduate who was home-schooled prior to attending a Christian college that has a 92% acceptance rate and is 60% white. He hadn't passed or even taken his MTEL license, which didn't matter as waivers and exceptions were made to get bodies off the street and into the classroom. While sounding like an indictment of my replacement, it spoke more to the times. Teachers were exiting the field in droves and especially the fields of math and science. My replacement had a biology background, and even if it was only in a few courses, it sure as hell beat the almost 50 years' time passage since my last bio class. He applied and was accepted, for that, he should be congratulated. It takes balls to want to be a teacher these days, so that's all I have to say about that.

My going back into the substitute general population didn't last long. Once again, Tori Mcknight found me with an assignment that she said that she and the administration only thought of me, to take over an ESL (English as a Second Language) class when the current teacher takes off for paternity leave. This would be different than teaching sheltered biology as the students were rated as 4's, meaning they could speak, read and write English at a decent proficiency but not yet well enough to pass their MTEL in the subject. And with my background as a writer, they (and I) all felt that this would be much more in my area of competence than biology. I agreed to meet with their current teacher, Kim Min-Jae as we had a prep period in common that day. He told me that he collected all cell phones before every class, and handed me the numbered caddy they were placed in. We were discussing my sitting in on his classes as he had about two weeks before his wife was expected to give birth and his anticipated departure of 6 weeks began, when his phone rang. As the son of an OB/GYN, I understood by his responses that his wife was going into labor right then. I told him to get his ass to the hospital and that was it, I had to take over that day for 4th period.

Both the A Day and B Day classes were similar. Period 1 had fewer students and they gave up their cell phones with no questions asked. They sat apart from each other and didn't talk during class at all, even if I asked them direct questions. Most of them did the work (all of it was on Canvas), and most of the work was exceptional. There were two students who were at opposite ends of the spectrum. Rene rarely came to class, and when she finally did, she argued loudly and disruptively, that she didn't belong there, and that her mother insisted that she take the class despite her strong protestations that her English was fine and that it was a waste of her time. Her argument did cause other students to chime in, basically telling her that if she was as proficient in English as she claimed, then she should just take the class and get the easy A. She scoffed at that notion and from that point on, she would come to class with about ten minutes left, sit down and go on her phone. I tried to argue that she still needed to hand me her phone out of fairness, but she flat refused, and a lesson I learned in year one, pick your battles on what hill you would be prepared to die on. If she wanted to flunk, thus proving her mother right and then be forced to take the class again and again, that was her deal.

The other student, Oscar, also challenged me on certain things, but they were always challenges that merited them. He was a straight A student who only railed against the status quo when he felt it required someone to speak up. I told him straight out to continue voicing his opinions, even when they contradicted mine as he wasn't doing it for the sake of being argumentative. That was a student I knew was going far in life, on the right path, and while he'll undoubtedly ruffle some feathers along the way, they would be feathers needing ruffling.

Period 2 for both the A and B days were more challenging, as they both contained students that didn't give up their phones so readily "*I'm charging it,*" was their most popular refrain, and they both had students that rarely attended class, and other students that you had to go to the mattresses to get them to do the work. I came upon a threat that worked somewhat for those students. As Kim Min-Jae was obviously a hardass, I reminded them that they would much rather have me correct their work as I would grade them on a curve. I would conclude that poor test results could be partially attributed to my not teaching the lessons well enough. That seemed to carry weight, especially as we were closing in on the end of my term there which would be at Christmas break.

Both period 4 classes had the type of knuckleheads you tear your hair out over. Period 4 A class had two students whose only goal was to get under my skin. They literally refused to not stop talking to each other, but WOULD continue to hit each other, or pound on their own chests like King Kong. One of them had the incredibly annoying habit of always making knocking sounds on his desk when there was a student out in the bathroom, and as nobody would let them back in upon their return, it was up to me to get up and open the door for them. No amount of yelling or threatening to call their dean, the biggest badass of the bunch; freshman dean, Ms. Kasey Capobianco, halted their behavior. There was also Lizzie, who seemed sweet enough, but so hated having to listen to my lectures or do any work, that she was constantly asking for bathroom passes or excuses to see the nurse, which amounted to her taking enough time out of class to claim legitimacy in her not finishing (or even starting) any of the assignments she needed to complete.

Period 4 B had two girls who so despised giving up their phones, that they burned holes into my head and told me that they hated me for it as their phones gave them joy and classwork didn't and how dare I have the unmitigated (well, they didn't use that word) gall (or that word) that I should confiscate the tools of which all their worldly satisfaction emanated. They would then talk throughout class and ignore my beseeching them to shut the heck (didn't use that word) up. There were also two Haitian girls in the class that were nice enough, but they would always sing in class, no matter how many times I reminded them that they weren't in choir. When I went to the whip, they would grudgingly do the assignments.

The part of the course that I ended up having to teach made little sense to me. First, there was the concept of noun clauses. I did extremely well in all my English classes in high school and college and many of my Amazon book reviews have extolled my virtues as a writer, but I couldn't identify every single noun clause given in examples if you had a gun to my head. And I never, ever wrote a sentence in one of my books where I thought to myself, *"OK, I need a noun clause here,"* or, *"Gee, I wonder where the noun clause is in THIS sentence?"* Noun clauses are just a thing. They exist, and I didn't understand why it was part of this curriculum. Get proficient enough at reading, writing and speaking English, and THEN worry about noun clauses.

The other part that took a ton of my time to convey, was how to write a summary. Now, when I was working on my PhD, I wrote a ton of summaries for the massive number of articles I had researched for my thesis. That's the only scenario where I think it's a good lesson to impart, but not on the various grades in high school where the students must get better with the basics. Every story that the curriculum had was about robots and AI. I guess that whoever dreamed up this lesson plan thought that children from Nicaragua, Guatemala, El Salvador, Brazil, and Haiti, to name a few, were so fascinated about robots and AI, that they would jump at the chance to read and summarize multiple articles about them. Not only did they have to write summaries, but the assignments also forced them to write a summary; revise the summary; edit the summary, and then write the final version. I knew beforehand when I read how all this was going down that all those versions would just be copied and pasted from their original version. Again, the good news for me was that summaries couldn't be corrected by the computer as all the multiple choice and fill-in-the-blanks were, and I used my exhortation of the classes wanting me to correct those assignments over their regular teacher to get the majority to complete them before the break started.

With the final days before Christmas break approaching and Kim Min-Jae would be returning to teach his classes. I thought about what the year (school year, that is), had brought. I was asked to teach multiple classes for extended periods that proved challenging, frightening and exhilarating. I had students tell me that I was terrible, but many more who gave me such positive feedback on what I tried to do that I will never forget them. There was Lonnie, one of the ELL students, whose IEP included autism and so many dos and don'ts regarding his class management, that I basically ignored them all and just went with my gut, to let him be and let him come to me. He was always ahead in his assignments and on the few times he needed help, he put up his hand and politely requested it. On our last day together, he did a high-five, fist and elbow bump and told me that I was one of his favorite teachers. There was Yunior, a muscular man-child from Haiti who had a megawatt smile and always shook my hand before and at the end of every class. Daniella, who was in my sheltered bio class, high-fives me whenever we see each other in the hallway, and asks me in decent English when I am coming back to her class. And I'll never forget Emily, the School Skipper who I see often in school these days and always has a huge smile for me whenever we bump into each other.

There are others that I might have said negative things about based on observations and interactions and that obviously included fellow teachers and other colleagues. While I don't regret or apologize for anything I've said here, I would like it to be known that if you work as an educator, or in any way in a school system, you, we, all of us are basically salmon, swimming upstream not just against the current, but against a tsunami of political, psychological, and physiological nonsense that continually tears at the fabric of what it is to be a public servant. I have nothing but the highest respect for everyone that makes this their career, and I am also very aware of my own idiosyncrasies, peccadillos, flaws, and personality traits that have, do, and will continue to rub people the wrong way. If I didn't mention you here, even with the name changes I installed, it's not because you didn't count or don't matter, or made no impression. I will never forget anyone that I have met here. It has been an unforeseen pleasure that I have been able to do this and hope to continue doing it for a few more years until I finally call it a career. I can't think of a better or more worthwhile coda to half a century of working in a variety of fields virtually all of which I didn't see coming, not as a child anyway. It's an impossible task to try and capture what goes on day-to-day in a school such as ours, and I hope that my limited viewpoint at least offered a glimmer of the hopes, dreams, failings, and everything else that goes with working in a high school that I now call home, filled with my children.

There are simply too many sights, sounds, and impressions I've come away with to include here. Some are haunting such as the crying from several of my students during the lockdown, the smile a student gives when you tell them how well they are doing in your class. Some can be complicated. I once saw a dean get into a student's grill when she was arriving late to school. When I had her in a class later that day and asked her about it, she told me that she has 5 brothers and sisters and that in order to be on time, she has to get up very early so she can take a shower, but her father yelled at her and told her not to do that again, so her choice was to make her father mad or come late to school. You hate yourself if for a second, you wonder if the student is shining you on, manipulating you, and you hate yourself for even thinking that, but the thought creeps in anyway. You know that on rainy or snowy or extremely cold days there will be significant absenteeism as there is no bus system to the school, and many students understandably don't want to get soaked or freeze during their walk. You learn that many students get depressed just before vacations as school is their only source for a hot meal. During the winter, you see so many students dressed for a season other than the one you're in as they are from tropical climates and can't afford things like winter clothes and jackets. On the mega-plus side, you see a lot of joy, and you hope that you're at least a tiny part of it, and then you get an email from a troubled student thanking you profusely for being there for them and you just want to hug them the next time you see them but you don't because you're afraid, and your emotions are in a blender, hoping that when you press stop, the joy modem is what's left.

I often tell the students that as I don't have any children or even nieces or nephews, they are like an alien race to me. And I badly want to be able to communicate with them and let them know that it's going to be alright, despite the madness surrounding them and you hate spouting platitudes. You really mean it, which is surprising as that is something you often couldn't even tell yourself, but with them you mean it. And you're grateful that you can say thank you in three languages.

Gracias

Obrigado

Merci

About The Author

Barry R Norman's books have received five-star reviews on Amazon. In addition to writing, he is also an award-winning filmmaker, film festival founder, former movie theater owner, and so-creator/writer/producer of the nationally syndicated, alternative music show, Cross Currents. Barry currently lives in Gloucester, MA having done tours of duty in Georgia, Florida, New York, Connecticut, Colorado and Maine.

Barry's writing influences are Jack Kerouac, Hunter Thompson, Kurt Vonnegut and Tom Wolfe. Kerouac's style of spontaneous prose was the one that stuck with him the most as it is also the method of filmmaking that he and his partner, iconic filmmaker/author Rick Schmidt use. It produces a visceral format which conveys the excitement, joys and pain he feels while producing the story.

His first book, *Flipping Point*, was begun by chance one day while sitting in his Maine movie theater, wondering about the existentialist situation he was in approaching his 59th birthday. He followed that up with three more books about different parts of his life – his childhood in *The Angriest Childhood in the World* followed by *The Delightful Denver Doldrums* which, departing from his first-person perspective to use a third-person tilt, details his years in Denver during his twenties. Finally, he wrote Counting Kitties, which deals with his lifelong problem of insomnia. Barry's next book was a huge departure from the hybrid novel/graphic novel, *Ambient Sanity*, with incredible illustrations by Brazilian artist, Jean Pedroso. Ambient Sanity investigates the thin line between sanity and genius as described with possible journeys into an alternate dimension.

We Blew It, is a partially comedic, historical analysis of all the smaller events and occurrences from 1969 to the present responsible for the shape of the United States and its fractured citizenry.

Finally, *Bad Day for Grandpa* is my *Collection of Short Stories and Other Drivel*.